PROTECTING YOUR MONEY

PROTECTING YOUR MONEY

BY
THEODORE E. HUGHES AND DAVID KLEIN

alyson books
los angeles | new york

© 1999 BY THEODORE E. HUGHES AND DAVID KLEIN. ALL RIGHTS RESERVED.

MANUFACTURED IN THE UNITED STATES OF AMERICA.

THIS TRADE PAPERBACK ORIGINAL IS PUBLISHED BY ALYSON PUBLICATIONS,
P.O. BOX 4371, LOS ANGELES, CALIFORNIA 90078-4371.
DISTRIBUTION IN THE UNITED KINGDOM BY TURNAROUND PUBLISHER SERVICES LTD.,
UNIT 3 OLYMPIA TRADING ESTATE, COBURG ROAD, WOOD GREEN,
LONDON N22 6TZ ENGLAND.

FIRST EDITION: JUNE 1999

99 00 01 02 03 **a** 10 9 8 7 6 5 4 3 2 1

ISBN 1-55583-498-1

CONTENTS

WHY THIS BOOK?

Although the basic concerns about personal finance and estate planning confronting gays and lesbians are identical to those of heterosexuals, there are significant societal and legal issues that make this book essential reading for members of the gay and lesbian community.

The legal problems are faced by all gays and lesbians. The social problems, on the other hand, because they involve family, friends, and sometimes employers or employees, will affect some individuals and not others. To a large extent, both the legal and the social problems can be alleviated through careful planning. And careful planning is what this book is all about.

■ THE LEGAL ISSUES

The legal prejudices faced by gays and lesbians are numerous and varied. For instance, increasing numbers of employers (both private and governmental) now offer domestic partnership benefits. State and federal tax laws, however, make no such allowances. No matter how stable or how long-lived the relationship, tax laws regard gay and lesbian couples as unrelated strangers. Consequently, a person enjoying benefits extended by his or her domestic partner's employer must pay income tax on these benefits. A straight, legally married spouse would not be similarly taxed.

Further discrimination is reflected in IRS rules governing dependency exemptions. In a marriage, one spouse may claim the other as a dependent no matter how much the dependent earns. If, however, one domestic partner wishes to claim the other as a dependent, the dependent partner must have an annual income of not more than $2,700, must receive at least 50% of his or her support from the partner claiming the dependency, and must be either a U.S. citizen or a resident of the United States, Canada, or Mexico.

Yet another example of government discrimination involves the "unlimited marital deduction" embodied in the federal gift and estate tax law. This deduction permits spouses—but not domestic partners—to make unlimited tax-free gifts to one another during their lives or at death. Domestic partners, on the other hand, cannot give one another more than $650,000 during life or at death without being subject to the federal gift and estate tax.[1]

Inheritance by a surviving domestic partner is also hampered by state law. State inheritance laws vary to some extent, but all specifically prohibit the total disinheritance of a legally married spouse and require that he or she receive a substantial portion of the deceased spouse's estate, regardless of the deceased's wishes. In the case of gay or lesbian domestic partners the opposite holds true. A surviving domestic partner receives none of the deceased's probate assets unless inheritance is specified in the deceased's will. And even this can be contested, sometimes successfully, usually by the deceased partner's parents or siblings. Further, state death taxes often discriminate against gays and lesbians by providing generous exemptions and lower rates for a legally married spouse receiving an inheritance from his or her deceased spouse, whereas no such considerations are provided for a surviving domestic partner.

In the absence of a will, trust, or contractual arrangement, state laws dictate how a deceased person's probate estate will be distributed. Although the share of the estate passing to the deceased's survivors varies, in all cases the spouse, children, parents, and siblings have priority. A surviving domestic partner—in the eyes of the law a total stranger—gets nothing. The various methods for protecting a surviving domestic partner against this kind of discrimination are dealt with in Chapters 1, 2, and 4.

In community-property states,[2] any earnings by either spouse become joint property, and either spouse has full control of half of the total assets. That control is retained even if the marriage is dissolved. This protection, which can be very important to a nonearning spouse, does not apply to domestic partners.

All of these issues, even if not immediately relevant to your particular situation, demonstrate the critical importance of executing a carefully drawn will and updating it periodically, subjects that will be dealt with in Chapter 1.

A gay or lesbian couple should also consider the possibility that their relationship, no matter how stable it seems at the moment, may at some future time disintegrate. Legally married straight couples face this same risk, but each spouse is protected by law against serious abuse because divorces are adjudicated in courts by judges who (presumably) order divisions of assets equitable to both parties. Because domestic partners enjoy no such legal protection, a domestic-partnership contract, discussed in Chapter 2, is an especially important consideration for gay and lesbian couples.

The following table summarizes the various ways in which the law discriminates in favor of legally married couples over gay and lesbian couples. As you can see, the differences are numerous and quite significant.

Significant Differences in the Law as it Relates to Legally Married Couples (Straight) Versus Gay and Lesbian Couples (Gay)

DURING THE LIFE OF BOTH PARTNERS	Straight	Gay
Eligibility for partner's employee benefits, such as life and health-care insurance, paid family leave, child-care, and prepaid legal services	Yes	No[1]
Federal income tax: Right (without limitation) to claim partner as an exemption	Yes	No

DURING THE LIFE OF BOTH PARTNERS	<u>Straight</u>	<u>Gay</u>
Right to file joint tax return	Yes	No
Subject to marriage tax penalty	Yes	No
Federal gift tax:		
Right to "unlimited marital deduction," which permits spouses to exchange unlimited tax-free gifts of any amount	Yes	No
Right to gift-splitting, which allows married couples to double the annual $10,000 gift-tax exclusion	Yes	No
Right to support from a partner during (and sometimes after) the relationship	Yes	No
Right to divorce-court protection if the relationship breaks up, temporarily or permanently	Yes	No
Right to visit partner in hospital or in prison	Yes	No
Right to make health-care decisions on behalf of an incapacitated partner	Yes	No
Preference to be appointed guardian/conservator of an incapacitated partner	Yes	No[2]
Right to purchase life insurance on a partner's life without demonstrating an insurable interest	Yes	No[3]

AFTER DEATH OF A PARTNER	<u>Straight</u>	<u>Gay</u>
Federal income tax:		
Ability to defer income tax on deceased spouse's IRA	Yes[4]	No
Federal estate tax:		
Right to "unlimited marital deduction," which permits spouses to transfer, at death, tax-free bequests of any amount	Yes	No
Eligibility for deceased partner's employee benefits, such as pension payments and bereavement leave	Yes	No
Eligibility for pension, burial, and survivor's pension:		
Social Security	Yes	No
Workers Compensation	Yes	No
Veterans Administration	Yes	No
Right to donate deceased partner's body/organs	Yes	No
Right to specify deceased partner's funeral/burial/cremation arrangements	Yes	No
Right to sue for and recover wrongful-death damages for loss of support, society, and companionship of deceased partner	Yes	No

DURING THE LIFE OF BOTH PARTNERS	Straight	Gay
Right to inherit partner's probate assets if partner dies intestate	Yes	No
Right to elect to take against deceased partner's will	Yes	No
Right to contest deceased partner's will if not named as a beneficiary	Yes	No

1. In recent years some employers have extended employee benefits to their employees' domestic partners, but this is currently the exception and not the rule.
2. In guardianship contests, the court will often appoint a spouse, parent, or adult child as guardian of an incapacitated partner, rather than appoint that person's domestic partner.
3. When purchasing an insurance policy on the life of a domestic partner, the purchaser is frequently required to show an "insurable interest" in the partner, for example, joint ownership of a home.
4. If a legally married person dies and leaves his IRA to a spouse, the spouse may roll over the amount received to his or her own IRA, thus no income taxes are due as a result of the IRA owner's death.

☐ **Next of Kin**

The "next of kin" concept is solidly embedded in the law, to be applied to the distribution of an estate when there is no valid will, and also in cases of illness or death. Gay and lesbian domestic partners are not legally considered kin. Consequently, in the event of a medical emergency, for example, a gay or lesbian domestic partner might not be admitted to visit his or her partner in an intensive-care unit or possibly even in a hospital room, and will definitely not have a say in whether the ill or injured partner is to be subject to "heroic measures" in an attempt to prolong life. Furthermore, a surviving gay or lesbian partner has no say whatsoever with respect to the donation of a deceased partner's organs, the choice of funeral rites, or the method or site of body disposal. Such lack of rights, however, can be overcome by signing a financial power of attorney and an advance directive, both described in Chapter 6.

THE SOCIAL ISSUES ■

Unlike legal issues, which affect all gays and lesbians, the relevance of social issues depends largely on an individual's relationship with his or her family. If the relationship is a good one, individuals are less likely to experience problems. If the relationship is strained (and sometimes even when it is not), the impact of judgmental or hostile parents and/or siblings can be devastating. In addition to parents and siblings, gay and lesbian couples may face hostility from numerous other sources, such as ex-spouses from "straight" marriages, children, employers, coworkers, neighbors, landlords, realtors, and any others with whom they have business dealings.

Although in recent years attitudes toward gays and lesbians have improved, there is no doubt that prejudice still exists. Consequently, a living will and a medical power of attorney, discussed in Chapter 6, are essential. Unfortunately, these legal documents, no matter how meticulously drafted, do not provide complete immunity against interference by parents, children, or siblings. Homophobic judges, on many occasions, have been sympathetic to parents or siblings contesting the will or other legal documents of a gay or lesbian individual. A revocable living trust, however, offers enhanced protection against family interference. This option is discussed in Chapter 4.

HOW TO USE THIS BOOK ■

Because the chapter titles are self-explanatory, this book can be read in any sequence, the reader choosing any chapter of immediate interest. Nevertheless, chapters have been arranged in a first-things-first sequence. Chapters 1 and 3—on wills and post-death instructions—deserve immediate attention. Similarly, Chapter 2, on living-together contracts, is relevant early on in a domestic partnership. Later chapters, on disability, death, and funeral arrangements, can—it is hoped—be postponed for many years, though it is never too early to begin planning.

■ A NOTE OF CAUTION

Although we have made every effort to ensure that the information in this book is accurate, comprehensive, and current, we cannot predict the ways in which both state and federal laws may change, nor can we take into account fully the specific problems with which you may be confronted in connection with your financial goals or your estate planning.

For this reason, you must not consider this book as your portable lawyer. Although the sample forms shown in the appendix can be used for general guidance, wills, trusts, and other estate-planning tools are complex documents that can be invalidated because of seemingly minor flaws or deviation from state law. The likelihood of invalidation increases when the social prejudices against homosexuality are factored into the equation. Hence, it is important that these documents be prepared—or at least checked—by a lawyer skilled in the intricacies of estate planning. This process will not be inordinately expensive if you come to a legal consultation with a comprehensive list of your assets, a clear notion of how you want to dispose of them, and any other information the lawyer is likely to need.

Notes

1 The 1997 Taxpayer Relief Act provides that gifts made after 1998 will be adjusted for inflation.

2 Arizona, California, Idaho, Louisiana, Nevada, New Mexico, Texas, Washington, and Wisconsin.

PART ONE

PERSONAL ISSUES

Chapter 1

YOUR WILL AND ITS SIGNIFICANCE

For many people, the act of preparing a will is their first confrontation with their own mortality. This is probably why they tend to procrastinate—and why three out of every four Americans die intestate (without a valid will). Yet a will, thoughtfully prepared, can do much to alleviate your fears about death, because it enables you to provide for the welfare of your loved ones after you are gone, and because it ensures that whatever probate estate[1] you leave behind will be distributed as you wish. Basically a will has three functions:

1) to nominate a guardian for your minor children (natural or adopted). If you have jointly adopted children,

your domestic partner will automatically assume custody, but, since there is the possibility you and your partner may die simultaneously, you may want to name an alternate guardian.

2) to specify who is to inherit how much and what portion of your estate; and

3) to name a personal representative (formerly known as an executor) who will make sure your estate is distributed according to the terms of your will.

These functions will be carried out regardless of whether you leave a will, but, if you die intestate, the decisions will be made by the local probate court in compliance with the laws of your state—and with consequences you would almost certainly find unacceptable.

If, for example, you and your domestic partner die simultaneously, the probate court will appoint a guardian for your minor children. In such circumstances the court is likely to appoint a relative, perhaps a sibling or parent, whose values and lifestyle may be very different from yours, whereas you might prefer a close friend or a different family member.

The loss of control associated with dying intestate applies not only to the care of minor children but to the disposition of whatever probate assets you leave. If you die without a will, the probate court will distribute your probate assets to your "heirs at law." Although inheritance laws vary from state to state, their common premise is that "blood is thicker than water." In other words, kinship is the fundamental principle governing the distribution of your probate estate. Thus, if you die intestate, your probate estate will go to your child or children—necessitating the appointment of a guardian, and possibly a conservator, if they are minors. And if they are not minors, they will inherit your assets even if they are alienated from you. If you die childless, your probate assets go to your parents or, if they are dead, to your siblings, and then nephews and nieces. If you leave no living relatives, your probate assets pass to the state. The crucial point here is that your domestic partner, whom the law regards as a total stranger, inherits nothing. Neither do any friends, stepchildren, or charities.

Laws of Intestacy Under the Uniform Probate Code

If Deceased is Survived[1] by:	Deceased's Probate Estate Distributed as Follows:
I(a) Spouse and Issue[2] (Born to Deceased and Spouse)	a) Spouse takes first $50,000 plus half of remainder[5] b) Issue share half of remainder
I(b) Spouse and Issue[2] (Born to Deceased alone)	a) Spouse takes half[5] b) Issue share half
II Spouse and Parents (No Issue)	a) Spouse takes first $50,000 plus half of remainder[2] b) Parents share half of remainder
III Spouse Only (No Issue)	Spouse takes all
IV Issue Only	Issue takes all
V Parents Only (No Spouse or Issue),	Parents take all

VI Parents' Issue[3] (No Spouse, Issue, or Parents)	Parents' Issue take all
VII Grandparents or their Issue[4] (No Spouse, Issue, Parents, Siblings)	a) Paternal grandparents or their Issue share half b) Maternal Grandparents or their Issue share half
VIII None of the above survive	c) State takes all[6]

[1]By at least 120 Hours
[2]Children, grandchildren, greatgrandchildren, etc.
[3]Deceased's brothers, sisters, nephews, nieces, grandnephews, grandnieces, etc.
[4]Deceased's uncles, aunts, first cousin's once removed etc.
[5]In addition, the spouse takes all of the deceased's community property.
[6]When the deceased is not survived by any persons in categories I thru VII, his or her intestate probate estate escheats to the state.

In the absence of a will, a personal representative appointed by the court must pay an annual bond premium (to protect against the personal representative's potential fraud or negligence), which will be charged against your estate. If, on the other hand, you name a personal representative in your will, you can specify that he or she is to serve without bond.

Since any one of these issues should convince you of the need to make a will as soon as possible, why is it that most Americans still die intestate? As we have noted, the real reason may be that making a will requires one to confront the prospect of one's own death, but, since admitting to a fear of death makes most people uncomfortable, other excuses are commonly offered. Here are some of them, along with some counterarguments:

Why think about it now? There's plenty of time.

Usually presented by young and middle-aged people, this argument overlooks the fact that death, especially by accident, heart attack, or the onset of a rapidly fatal disease, can occur at any time. Furthermore, it is people in the younger age group who are most likely to leave minor children. Since an accident may kill both domestic partners simultaneously, only a will can ensure that the person appointed as guardian of your children and conservator or trustee of your children's assets will be someone you like and trust.

My net worth isn't high enough to justify the trouble and expense.

Actually most people underestimate their net worth, not realizing what inflation has done to the value of their real estate, automobiles, stock portfolio, collection of antiques, and other possessions. Moreover, there is no way to estimate accurately what your net worth will be at the time of your death—or even afterward. It is possible you might die shortly after receiving a large inheritance or while holding a winning lottery ticket. Or you may die in an accident or in surgery, resulting in a successful lawsuit for damages arising from your death through someone's negligence. Or one of your stocks, whose value has been negligible for years, might suddenly "take off."

Why can't I put all my property into joint ownership with my domestic partner so it will pass automatically to him or her when I die?

Joint ownership, discussed in Chapter 4, can be useful because it avoids probate. But it should be used only if your relationship with your partner is thoroughly stable since, once established, joint ownership may be very difficult to dissolve. Moreover, it rarely covers all your assets and possessions. Are your cars owned jointly? (They should not be.) What about your collections of clocks and Japanese prints? Does the bill of sale for that antique Chippendale table list both of you as owners? Are there securities you or your broker neglected to register in joint ownership? Even the most carefully planned estate is likely to include property that is yours and yours alone. Unless such probate assets are willed to a specified beneficiary, the probate court will distribute them according to state law.

You must also be concerned about what happens to your jointly held assets should you and your partner be killed simultaneously, or if one of you survives but dies later without having made a will.

■ WHAT A WILL CAN DO

Here, in summary, are some of the issues a will can resolve.

A will can name a guardian and an alternate guardian for your minor children. If the assets being left to a minor are too substantial or too complicated for the guardian to manage, your will can also name a conservator to manage the assets until your child reaches the age of majority (18 in most states).

A will can name a personal representative to manage your estate until it is finally distributed. Unlike a court-appointed personal representative, one named in your will may be relieved from the requirement of purchasing a bond, thus saving your estate the cost of bond premiums.

A will can designate your primary and contingent beneficiaries: "I give $20,000 to A if he (she) survives my death; otherwise to B."

A will can specify charitable gifts: "I leave $10,000 to Brown University, and $5,000 to the American Humane Society."

A will can make conditional gifts: "I give $10,000 to my nephew, Steven Cort, provided he has earned his baccalaureate degree by the time of my death."

A will can forgive a debt. If, for example, A owes you $5,000, your will can specify that you forgive any balance outstanding at the time of your death.

A will can establish a trust and name a trustee for minor children, aged or incompetent persons, or any other beneficiary to ensure that person gets the benefit of whatever part of your estate you designate, but not the responsibility for managing it. Will-created trusts such as these are called "testamentary" trusts, and can be used to postpone distribution of all or part of an inheritance beyond the time when a beneficiary reaches the age of majority—to age 25, for example—so the beneficiary will be more mature and less likely to waste his or her inheritance. In the absence of a testamentary trust, a child will have access to his or her total inheritance upon reaching the age of majority.

A will can transfer some or all of your probate assets to a living trust established during your lifetime. Living trusts are covered in Chapter 4.

A will can revoke all previous wills.

It should be noted that wills must express clear, unambiguous instructions, not merely wishes or hopes. Thus, "I wish my friend John to receive my clock" is an unclear and probably unenforceable version of "I give John Howard my Chauncey Jerome banjo clock."

■ WHAT A WILL CAN'T—OR SHOULDN'T—DO

Because most people have learned what they know about wills from news stories, movies, novels, or television, it's not surprising they have picked up a good deal of misinformation. There are several provisions that should not be included in a will, either because they will not be carried out by the probate court on grounds they are illegal or against public policy, or because they are simply inadvisable.

Here are some examples:

A will may not place a condition on a bequest if the condition is generally seen as contrary to sound social policy. Thus, you may not leave a bequest to a brother "provided that he divorce Susan Arbuthnot, to whom he is now married." The probate court would hold that disruption of a marriage is not sound social policy and therefore the condition would be unenforceable. Similarly, provisions bequeathing gifts to illegal organizations, such as terrorist groups, may be successfully contested. On the other hand, a bequest to an organization that advocates same-sex marriage is perfectly legal, since, although same-sex marriage is not legal, it is not illegal either. (In the eyes of the law, same-sex marriage simply does not exist.)

A will may disinherit a child, but the disinherited child should be named specifically. Otherwise the child may claim he or she was omitted inadvertently and is thus entitled to whatever portion of the estate he or she would have inherited had the parent died intestate. This is an argument that has been made successfully on numerous occasions. It is unwise to disinherit anyone by bequeathing him or her the sum of one dollar. Before an estate may be closed, all beneficiaries must sign receipts for their inheritances. If the beneficiary thus insulted refuses to cooperate, a problem is created for your personal representative.

A will may not force a gift on an indifferent or unwilling recipient. A beneficiary is under no obligation to accept anything left to him by the will. Thus, if you wish to leave your national champion St. Bernard to your good friend Jane De-Voto, you'd best consult with her first.

In some (but not all) states a will may not impose penalties on someone who chooses to contest it. In those states, a condition such as "I give my son Jonathan $5,000, but if he contests my will I direct that he shall receive nothing," will not be enforced if the probate court feels his lawsuit contesting the will has merit. Similarly, a will may not require anyone contesting the will to pay litigation costs incurred by the estate. This restriction can be especially frustrating for gays and lesbians, particularly those alienated from their families—who might be more inclined than normal to contest the will.

There is no restriction against specifying funeral arrangements in a will, but these directions may be frustrated if the will is not located and read immediately upon death. (Chapter 7 suggests a more reliable procedure for making your wishes known.)

Although a will may specify that some of your possessions are to be given to designated beneficiaries, it generally should not contain a complete inventory of your assets, since any change in these would necessitate a revision of your will. Assets should be inventoried in your Letter of Instruction, described in Chapter 3.

You may, if you like, include in your will whatever statement of philosophy or "message to the world" you choose, but it is unwise to use your will as a vehicle for venting displeasure with or animosity against specifically named individuals, since if the will is probated, it becomes a public document available to anyone who wants to read it. Any scurrilous attacks it contains will, at best, embarrass your survivors and, at worst, involve your estate in the expensive defense of a libel suit brought by the injured party.

■ WHO SHOULD PREPARE THE WILL?

The foregoing list of dos and don'ts is not intended to encourage you to embark on a do-it-yourself will. On the contrary, it illustrates that a significant number of details, many of them seemingly petty, can render invalid, in whole or in part, a will prepared without competent professional advice. For example, many people believe you can make a will simply by writing out your instructions in longhand and affixing your signature. Aside from the technical errors it may contain, such a will, known as a holographic (hand-written) will, has no legal standing whatsoever in almost half the states. In some circumstances, however, it may be better than no will at all. Oral wills, such as deathbed statements, are even less widely accepted. Tape recordings, sound or video, are not valid as wills at all because they are not considered "writings."

State Requirements Governing Wills

	Minimum Age to Make a Will	Number of Required Witnesses	Recognizes Holographic Wills	Recognizes Oral Wills	Conditions Imposed On Oral Wills*
Alabama	18	2	No	No	
Alaska	18	2	Yes	No	
Arizona	18	2	Yes	No	
Arkansas	18	2	Yes	No	
California	18	2	Yes	No	
Colorado	18	2	Yes	No	
Connecticut	18	2	No	No	
Delaware	18	2	No	No	
District of Columbia	18	2	No	Yes	6,7,8,12,16
Florida	18	2	No	No	
Georgia	14	2	No	Yes	7,12,17,19
Hawaii	18	2	No	No	
Idaho	18	2	Yes	No	
Illinois	18	2	No	No	
Indiana	18	2	No	Yes	3,4,6,9,11 12,17,19,21
Iowa	18	2	No	No	
Kansas	18	2	No	Yes	6,7,12,17
Kentucky	18	2	Yes	No	
Louisiana	16	2	Yes	No	
Maine	18	2	Yes	No	
Maryland	18	2	Yes	No	
Massachusetts	18	2	No	Yes	6,8
Michigan	18	2	Yes	No	
Minnesota	18	2	No	No	
Mississippi	18	2	Yes	Yes	7,10,12,19
Missouri	18	2	No	Yes	2,6,11,12, 17,19,21
Montana	18	2	Yes	No	
Nebraska	19	2	Yes	No	
Nevada	18	2	Yes	Yes	3,7,12,17,19
New Jersey	18	2	Yes	No	
New Mexico	18	2	No	No	
New York	18	2	Yes	Yes	9,12,20
North Carolina	18	2	Yes	Yes	7,12,16,19
North Dakota	18	2	Yes	No	
Ohio	18	2	No	Yes	7,12,14,16,19
Oklahoma	18	2	Yes	Yes	3,8,11,12
Oregon	18	2	No	No	
Pennsylvania	18	2	Yes	No	
Rhode Island	18	2	No	No	
South Carolina	18	3	No	Yes	7,10,13,19

South Dakota	18	2	Yes	No	
Tennessee	18	2	Yes	Yes	
Texas	18	2	Yes	Yes	7,10,13,19
Utah	18	2	Yes	No	
Vermont	18	2	Yes	Yes	1,6,15,19
Virginia	18	2	Yes	Yes	6,8
Washington	18	2	No	Yes	3,5,6,7,12, 17,19
West Virginia	18	2	Yes	Yes	6,8
Wisconsin	18	2	No	No	
Wyoming	18	2	Yes	No	

*Key to Conditions Imposed on Oral Wills

1. Limited to $200.
2. Limited to $500.
3. Limited to $1,000.
4. Limited to $10,000.
5. Unlimited if testator is in military service.
6. Limited to only personal property.
7. Available only during last illness.
8. Testator must be in military service.
9. Testator must be in military service during wartime.
10. Testator must be at home or other place of death.
11. Testator must be in contemplation or fear of death.
12. Requires two witnesses.
13. Requires three witnesses.
14. Witnesses must not be beneficiaries of will.
15. Must be reduced to writing within 6 days.
16. Must be reduced to writing within 10 days.
17. Must be reduced to writing within 30 days.
18. Must be reduced to writing within 60 days.
19. Must be probated within 6 months following death.
20. Expires 1 year after testator's discharge from service.
21. Cannot be used to revoke a written will.

Must you, then, pay for the services of a lawyer? Or can you make your own will by using the forms provided in the appendix, or in a number of "how to make a will" books? Unfortunately, there is no unequivocal answer to this question. Most practicing lawyers would caution you against the do-it-yourself alternative—just as most of them are unenthusiastic about the simplified do-it-yourself divorce procedure—but one can hardly assume their advice is entirely disinterested. The make-your-own-will books are, after all, typically written by lawyers at least as competent as a general practitioner who does not specialize in estate planning.

On the other hand, problems can arise not because the do-it-yourself manuals are defective, but because readers are careless in following the instructions or are unable to apply the general instructions to specific, occasionally exceptional situations.

A few states (California and Michigan, for example) offer the public a simple, fill-in-the-blanks "statutory will" form that complies with the laws of the state. We suggest you inquire about the availability of such a form in your state at the local probate court or your state's bar association if this possibility interests you.

Our advice is that if your assets are not substantial or complicated, and if the provisions you intend to put in your will are fairly conventional, and if you have the time and patience to read and follow sometimes complicated instructions, you may safely write your own will, using a book on the subject or perhaps the form we provide in the appendix.[2] But these are rather significant ifs, and you may decide that the relatively modest cost of professional preparation is a bargain in terms of the sense of security it can provide.

WHAT YOUR LAWYER NEEDS TO KNOW ■

Although fees for preparation of a will vary widely from one lawyer to another, all lawyers earn a living by selling their time. Thus, your bill is likely to be smaller if you arrive at your lawyer's office with all the information he or she is likely to need. A complete listing of your assets, for example, will not only circumvent a lengthy question-and-answer session but will avoid omissions and oversights requiring subsequent visits or telephone calls. You may, when you enter your lawyer's office, have only a vague idea of what a "contingent beneficiary" is, but you ought to have clearly in mind all the individuals to whom you intend to leave a portion of your estate.

Here is a list of information your lawyer will need for the preparation of even the simplest will.

1) Your Personal Representative

Be prepared to name someone who will, on your death, see to it that your probate assets are collected and inventoried, your legitimate debts paid, your probate assets distributed according to your wishes, and your estate closed. If your estate is large and/or complex, you may prefer a personal representative with experience in estate management—a bank or a trust company, for example. But bear in mind that personal representatives are entitled to a fee ranging from one to five percent of the value of your estate. Moreover, personal representatives must be bonded. Both the fee and the annual bond premium are paid with funds from your estate.

If your estate is fairly simple, you may want to choose as your personal representative your domestic partner, a trusted friend, or a member of your family. It is perfectly acceptable to select one of your beneficiaries as your personal representative, provided you foresee no conflict of interest. Whoever you choose should be younger, or at least no older than you and possess integrity, good judgment, and reasonable competence in ordinary business transactions. Many states require that a personal representative be an adult resident of your state.

A friend or relative who serves as personal representative may choose to waive his or her fee, and, unless you feel that bonding will protect your estate against his or her possible negligence, your will can stipulate he or she may serve without bond. Furthermore, if you choose a trusted and competent personal representative, you can give that person considerably more authority to settle your affairs than is given court-appointed personal representatives by the laws of most states.

Obviously you should get an individual's consent to serve as your personal representative before naming him or her in your will. And if you choose an individual rather than a bank or a trust company, be prepared to name an alternate, since the first-named personal representative may not outlive you or may become unable or unwilling to assume the responsibility. Banks and trust companies, on the other hand, are "immortal" and consequently more dependable. Nevertheless, banks and trust companies might not be the best possible choice for a small or simple estate. Because their fee is often a percentage of the estate, they may not be motivated to work as quickly or efficiently in closing a small estate as they would in closing a large one.

2) Guardian and Conservator for Minor Children

If you have minor children, either natural or adopted, your will should name a guardian for them—someone who will take over your role as parent until each
child reaches the age of majority. You may have read
novels or seen movies in which the 12-year-old daughter heroically undertakes the rearing of her younger
siblings, but the truth of the matter is that your minor
children cannot be enrolled in school, consent to medical treatment, or make important financial decisions
except through an adult guardian appointed by the
probate court to act on their behalf. (You probably
wouldn't want your minor child, no matter how mature, making these decisions, anyway.) Consequently,
the probate court will select a guardian if your will fails
to nominate one.

If your minor child has been adopted by both you
and your domestic partner, you should select a
guardian who will serve in the event that you and your
partner die simultaneously. If, on the other hand, the
adoption was not joint, you will probably want to nominate your domestic partner as guardian and then another individual as an alternate guardian should you
and your partner die simultaneously. The same procedure holds true for a natural-born child. It should be
noted that, if the child is your natural child from a previous "straight" marriage or partnership and you have
custody, the child's custody reverts, on your death, to
the noncustodial natural parent. Even if you have

named your gay or lesbian partner as guardian in your will, a surviving natural parent challenging that provision is likely to succeed.

In general, the guardian, unlike the personal representative, need not be a resident of your state. You may choose a relative or perhaps a close friend. Some parents of teenage children draw up a list of three or four persons as acceptable guardians and permit the children to make a choice. Some parents choose an adult child as guardian for their minor children, but this can be risky. Even if the current sibling relationship is very sound, the sudden increase in authority endowed by the guardianship can threaten it.

In all states, a child, upon reaching the age of 14, has the right to veto the parent's choice of a guardian and to nominate a substitute. If the probate court agrees the proposed substitution is in the child's best interests, the parent's will-specified nomination may be defeated.

Your principal criteria in choosing a guardian are likely to include the guardian's personality, ethical standards, and child-rearing style, as well as his or her current relationship with your children. Financial stability, though, cannot be entirely disregarded. Guardians are entitled to reimbursement from the child's inheritance for reasonable costs incurred in maintaining and educating the child, and providing medical and other services. But since the cost of rearing a child from infancy through college is estimated at more than $100,000, anyone undertaking a guardianship takes on a potentially substantial financial burden, especially if the child's inheritance is limited. This burden can be lessened through careful planning, including the purchase of life insurance. Nevertheless, you will certainly want to obtain in advance the consent of anyone you plan to nominate.

If you have a larger estate that will provide amply for your children, a second question arises: who should control their inheritance—not only to oversee disbursements for expenses incurred by the guardian in the raising of your child, but also to conserve or increase the inheritance through effective investment. The person you select for this role is called a conservator. You may, if you wish, choose the same person to serve as both guardian and conservator (and, for that matter, as personal representative), but since skill in child-rearing is not necessarily related to financial acumen, you may wish to appoint a separate conservator—perhaps a bank. The conservator, like the personal representative, is entitled to a fee for managing the child's estate.

The responsibility of the conservator terminates automatically when the child reaches the age of majority. If you have left your children a substantial amount of money and if you think that, at age 18, your child is not likely to be mature enough to manage his or her inheritance wisely, you can, in your will, set up a trust specifying that the child not have access to the trust assets until reaching whatever age you choose. In the interim, the trust assets will be managed by a trustee of your choice. The trustee fulfills the functions of a conservator, but without the time limits and various other restrictions imposed on a conservator. Trusts are covered in more detail in Chapter 4.

3) Beneficiaries

Although you undoubtedly know whom you intend to designate as your primary beneficiaries—presumably your domestic partner, your children, and perhaps a friend, parent, or favorite niece or nephew—it is important to have in mind several contingent beneficiaries. A contingent beneficiary is "next in line" should a primary beneficiary die before you or refuse to accept your gift. For example, even though your children are already primary beneficiaries, you can stipulate that whatever portion of your estate you have willed to your domestic partner or any other person is to go to your children, not necessarily in equal shares, should that person predecease you.

But what if a married daughter—even though she is 30 years younger than you—should predecease you? Do you want her share to go to your son-in-law or to a trust set up for your daughter's children, with someone appointed as trustee? These specifics should be clearly spelled out in your will.

Lawyers are not congenital pessimists, but they are trained to identify contingencies, no matter how improbable. Although it is highly unlikely—short of a catastrophe at a family reunion—that most of your primary beneficiaries will die before you, you ought to provide your lawyer with at least two levels of contingency for each separate gift. For example, "I give $10,000 to A, provided he survives me, otherwise to B, provided she survives me, otherwise to C."

Given the decreasing size of families, the dispersal of the extended family, and the possibility of alienation of some family members, you may find yourself running out of relatives before you have exhausted all possible contingencies. Bear in mind, however, that if all your contingencies become exhausted, and if you do not have any surviving blood relatives to step forward and claim your probate estate, the residue is forfeited to the state treasury. This can be avoided by adding as contingent beneficiaries friends, charities, or other organizations.

4) Specific Monetary Bequests

Because you may not die for many years after making your will, you have no way of accurately estimating the ultimate value of your probate estate. This is of little consequence if you have only two or three primary beneficiaries, because in such circumstances you are likely to specify your bequests in terms of percentages or fractions of the total estate. For example, you might leave 75% to your domestic partner, specifying that the remaining 25% be divided equally among your surviving children.

If you have a number of small bequests, however, you need to decide whether to express these gifts in dollars or percentages. If, for example, you'd like to leave a favorite nephew $1,000, which currently represents 1% of your estate, should you describe the bequest as "$1,000" or as "1% of my estate?" If, 20 years from now, inflation shrinks the purchasing value of $1,000 by 80 percent, the gift becomes insultingly small. On the other hand, 1% of your estate may at the time of your death represent an amount much larger than you intended. There is no general answer to the dollars-versus-percentage issue, but it needs to be considered for each of your smaller bequests and reconsidered each time you revise your will.

5) Specific Property Gifts

You may want to give certain of your possessions, large or small, to specific people, whether or not they are beneficiaries of other gifts. Your quilt collection, for example, might be given to a fellow quilter. Your grandmother's gold brooch might be given to your daughter rather than to your son. If, before you die, any of these things pass from your possession— through a lifetime gift, a fire, or theft, for example— you need not revise your will. The gift "fails," and the named beneficiary will have no claim against your probate estate.

6) Complete List of Assets

Although a complete inventory of your assets does not belong in your will (because it is likely to change significantly before you die), it is useful to draw one up to show your lawyer before he or she draws up your will. To begin with, the inventory will provide your lawyer with a general idea of how complex your will needs to be. In addition, if your estate is a large one, he or she may have suggestions for avoiding taxes and other problems—a subject dealt with in Chapters 4 and 9.

If you feel uncomfortable disclosing to your lawyer the full extent of your assets because you suspect he or she will not keep the information confidential, you ought to find another lawyer. Making a will is a "moment of truth," and concealing relevant information can only frustrate your plan and jeopardize the interests of your beneficiaries.

Your lawyer, and almost certainly your domestic partner, should be included in your "circle of confidentiality" with respect to your will. Inclusion of anyone else is a matter you should consider carefully. On the other hand, you may want to elicit specific preferences from some of your primary beneficiaries about particular possessions. You might also want to discuss with your alma mater or any other institutional beneficiary the specific terms of a bequest. Generally speaking, though, your will is a very personal affair.

EXECUTING AND PROTECTING YOUR WILL ∎

Armed with the information described in the preceding pages, you should be able to answer whatever questions your lawyer asks. The technical details of compliance with state law can then be left to him or her. The next step is for you to read the draft of the will—at home, relaxed, and preferably in consultation with your domestic partner—to make certain the will accurately reflects your intent. Signing the will is best done in your lawyer's office, because he or she will be familiar with state requirements for signing and witnessing. There is no need for the witnesses to read the will—they are witnessing only your signature—although they must understand that what they are signing is your will.

Some lawyers draft wills that nominate themselves or their firms as the personal representative or as the lawyer who will be employed to probate the will. There is no reason for you to commit your estate to employing a specific lawyer. You might move from the community or change lawyers for any number of reasons, and a specific commitment would then require revision of your will.

You will receive several copies of your will, but you should sign only the original. This will eliminate the need to find and destroy multiple copies if you later decide to revise or revoke your will. The signed original should be kept where it is (1) safe against fire, theft, or other loss; (2) readily retrievable by you; and (3) readily located by your survivors after your death. The storage location that probably best meets these criteria is the will depository maintained by most county probate courts. For a nominal one-time filing fee, you can file the will for safekeeping until it is probated or revoked. During your lifetime, only you have access to it. On your death it becomes available to your survivors for use in the probate process.

Storing a will in a safe deposit box is also a common practice. In some states, however, your bank, on hearing of your death, is required by law to seal your box until a representative of the state treasury can inventory its contents for tax purposes. In such circumstances, your survivors will need to apply for a court order permitting them to retrieve the will.

Storing the will at home along with other important papers is a common practice as well, but a desk drawer or filing cabinet may provide insufficient privacy and/or protection against fire and theft. Storing your will in your lawyer's office, as some lawyers recommend, may place you in an awkward position if you subsequently establish a relationship with a different lawyer. Moreover, if your lawyer has possession of your will, your survivors may feel an obligation to employ that lawyer when, in fact, they would prefer to use another.

■ MODIFYING OR REVOKING YOUR WILL

As we have noted, it is important to make a will early in life, because death can occur at any time. But the statistical probability is that you will live for many years after executing your will. Thus, many of the circumstances on which you based your original will may change. The value and complexity of your assets, for example, may increase. A beneficiary may die; a beneficiary's needs may increase or diminish; your feelings toward a beneficiary may change drastically. You may separate from your domestic partner; you may adopt a child; or you may want (or need) to change your original choice of personal representative, guardian, conservator, or trustee. It is also possible you will move to another state. Not all states recognize the validity of a will executed when you lived elsewhere, and even in states that do, your will may require revisions to comply with the new state's laws. Obviously, then, a will is not something you can execute and then put away with a sigh of relief. It requires periodic review, and each review may lead to minor changes or major revisions.

Like your original will, changes and revisions should be made promptly and not put off on the grounds that you are currently in good health. Bear in mind that a will can be executed or changed only when you are mentally competent, and that mental incompetence—as a consequence of senility, mental illness, or coma caused by injury or disease—may precede your death by many years. In such circumstances, a guardian may need to be appointed to handle your business affairs, but a guardian does not have the power to change or revoke your will.

Codicils □

If your will requires only a minor revision—a change in the amount you've bequeathed to a specific beneficiary, for example, or the addition of a gift to a charitable organization, or a change in the designation of a personal representative or guardian—you can make the change by means of a codicil, which is simply an amendment to the original will. Like the will, a codicil must comply with state law for witnessing and other formalities, and it will be probated together with the will.

Although there is no limit to the number of changes that can be embodied in a codicil, or even the number of codicils that can accompany a will, the presence of a large number of codicils can complicate the probate process. Hence, there is a point at which it is better to revise the entire will rather than add another codicil. Revising your will is essentially similar to the preparation of the original will.

☐ Revocation

There are several ways in which your current will can be revoked. You can, at any time, simply destroy it (or instruct someone to destroy it in your presence). This, however, leaves you without a will. A better method is to execute a new will that revokes all previous wills. The most efficient way to manage your affairs is to update your will periodically by signing a codicil or a new will. If you do this conscientiously, your will should accurately reflect your most recently expressed wishes.

■ AVOIDING WILL CONTESTS

Will contests may be more frequent in the estates of gays and lesbians if their parents, siblings, or adult children are hostile or alienated. This possibility increases if the estate is substantial. A will may be contested by anyone who is by the terms of the will, or who would be by law if the deceased had died intestate, entitled to a share of the estate. Such person may allege that he or she was deprived of his or her share in the estate because of some defect in the testator (the person making the will), in the will, or in the circumstances surrounding its execution. (Grounds for contesting a will are detailed in Chapter 9.) Thus, it is important when the will is being executed to make it as contest-proof as possible.

Will contests are typically filed only if the deceased leaves probate assets. Thus, if assets are held in nonprobatable form, a contest is far less likely. An effective way to reduce or eliminate probate assets is to place them in a revocable living trust, described in Chapter 4. Assets held in such a trust remain under your control as long as you are alive and competent, but on your death they pass into the control of a "successor trustee," whom you have chosen. Since the assets no longer belong to you, they are beyond the control of your will. Consequently a will contest will not benefit the contestant. In rare instances a trust may be contested, but such actions are infrequent and rarely successful.

Another tactic is the titling of one's assets in joint ownership, which, on the death of one joint owner, causes the assets to pass automatically to the surviving owner. Since jointly held assets are unaffected by a will, there is less likelihood of a contest. Joint ownership, however, is not without inherent problems, noted in Chapter 4.

If neither of these alternatives is acceptable, a number of steps can be taken when the will is executed to protect against a successful will contest. For example, the signing of a will may be recorded on videotape, at which point in the proceedings the lawyer can engage the testator in conversation to demonstrate his or her soundness of mind and freedom from undue influence.

In addition, your lawyer can solicit (and retain in his or her files) reports about the testator's competence from physicians, psychiatrists, and any other qualified person who had contact with and knowledge about the testator at or about the time of the will signing. It is wise, too, to select witnesses to the signing who are younger than the testator, disinterested, credible, and whose whereabouts are likely to remain known so they can be called upon to testify in defense of the will should a contest develop.

■ THE PROBLEM OF PROBATE

Throughout this chapter we have made glancing references to the probate court and the probate administration of estates without explaining either of them in detail. The reason for this is that the drafting of a will is essentially a personal matter, whereas probate deals largely with financial issues. Hence, the probate process and the various ways of avoiding probate will be discussed in Chapters 4 and 9.

Notes

1   Your probate estate consists of assets in your name alone that, on your death, re quire administration by the probate court (See Chapter 9). Your probate estate need not include all your assets and may, in fact, include none of them.
2   Nolo Press has published Willmaker, software that allows the user to prepare a state-specific will. The manual accompanying this software is, in itself, a useful guide to the complexities of will-preparation.

Chapter 2

DOMESTIC-PARTNERSHIP CONTRACTS, CHILD-RELATED ISSUES, AND ADULT ADOPTION

B ecause state laws do not recognize gay and lesbian domestic partnerships as legitimate, your relationship is not afforded the protections available to legally married couples with respect to ownership and inheritance of property, divorce decrees, support obligations, custody of children, and taxation of income. This chapter will address these issues, suggesting tactics for legitimizing your domestic partnership.

There are four basic methods gay and lesbian domestic partners can employ to give their relationship a legal status affording at least some of the rights and benefits available to legally married straight couples.

First, as we noted in Chapter 1, domestic partners can execute wills designating each other as beneficiaries.

Second, as we also noted in Chapter 1, and will cover in more detail in Chapters 4 and 6, gay and lesbian partners can designate one another as beneficiaries of a trust, and sign financial and medical durable powers of attorney in favor of each other.

Third, gay and lesbian couples can reinforce their partnership by executing a domestic-partnership contract, specifying each partner's respective rights and responsibilities. Furthermore, domestic-partnership status can be registered in a growing number of municipalities.[1]

A fourth option is for one partner to take full responsibility for the other through a process known as adult adoption.

■ THE DOMESTIC-PARTNERSHIP CONTRACT

The domestic-partnership contract is an extremely useful device that is coming into increasingly widespread acceptance. Sometimes called a cohabitation or living-together agreement, the domestic-partnership contract is similar to the prenuptial or nuptial agreement used by engaged or legally married straight couples. Many gay or lesbian partners, like many legally or soon to be legally married heterosexual partners, hesitate to sign a domestic-partnership contract on the grounds that executing such a document implies a lack of trust, destroys the spontaneity of the relationship, or is simply unromantic. Others, even though they own property jointly or adopt children jointly, feel the time and expense involved in preparing the contract is simply not worth the benefits to be achieved.

Despite these reservations, however, there are several good reasons for signing a domestic-partnership contract. A major automobile accident, for example, can wreak legal and financial havoc if it results in the disability or death of one of the partners. Or a partner's rights may be challenged by public officials, landlords, hostile relatives, school officials, welfare workers, or medical personnel. Or, worse, a dispute may thrust the unwed couple into court. In all such situations, the domestic partners' legal status is more firmly established when the status of their familial relationship is clearly documented by a domestic-partnership contract. Furthermore, the existence of a domestic-partnership contract can deter or prevent litigation between partners in the event of a dispute or break-up.

Because current laws favor the status of legally married couples, gay or lesbian domestic partners face difficulties in establishing the legal legitimacy of their relationship and their rights as a family unit. These rights can be significantly enhanced by a document specifying each partner's relationship to the other, to their minor children, and to their solely and co-owned property.

Domestic partners are ineligible to file for divorce or annulment. Consequently, neither partner can rely on a court of law for decisions regarding the equitable division of property, the occupancy and disposition of a dwelling, or child support, visitation, and custody. A clearly written domestic-partnership contract spelling out a couple's marriage-like relationship and personal, financial, and custodial understandings can do much to avoid disagreements, litigation, and financial loss.

The decision to sign a domestic-partnership contract is not an easy one. To begin with, it is unlikely both partners will approach the project with the same level of enthusiasm. Indeed, one partner may suspect the other of mistrust, greed, or anticipation that the relationship will be of short duration. In addition, candidly discussing the contract may bring into sharp focus and, possibly, contention economic disparities between the partners.

Nevertheless, the fact that many legally married couples, even though they do not face the many legal disadvantages encountered by gay or lesbian domestic partners, find domestic-partnership contracts useful should encourage you to seriously consider this option. The fact that some municipalities have established domestic-partnership ordinances granting rights and responsibilities[2] to same-sex couples should provide further inducement to you to confirm your relationship in writing.

□ What a Domestic-Partnership Contract Should Include

A domestic-partnership contract should include a functional definition of the concept of family and the relationship of each partner to this concept. If minor children are involved, it should also specify who has obligations of child support and rights of custody and visitation.

In addition, the contract should outline rights to any property acquired by either of the partners before the partnership was established; in the absence of a contract, property owned by one partner before the cohabitation began belongs to him or her alone. Similarly, the question of who owns property acquired since the cohabitation began—and its disposition in the event of a break-up—should also be resolved. Assets acquired jointly, such as a car bought with the funds of both partners, belong to both partners. But if, after a break-up, a dispute results, a court may have to decide the issue of ownership, since most assets (including cars) cannot be split in two. In such a situation, a domestic-partnership contract specifying the division of all co-owned assets could resolve any dispute without the expense, delay, and angst of litigation.

As we have noted earlier, in community property states each member of a legally married couple is, on dissolution of the marriage, automatically entitled to half of all assets acquired during the marriage, regardless of which spouse actually acquired them. But, since a domestic partnership does not enjoy the legal status of a marriage, a domestic-partnership contract should be utilized to specify the ownership, use, and maintenance of partnership assets.

The domestic-partnership contract should also recite the degree of support, if any, each partner owes the other. In the absence of a contract, neither partner has any legal obligation to support the other. The contract can be used to specify a degree of support, both during the partnership and after a break-up, or that neither partner has any obligation to support the other.

Domestic-partnership contracts should address the intentions and resources of each partner. Consequently, no sample contract form could possibly take into account all the issues a couple might want to consider, nor should domestic partners necessarily use as a model the nuptial agreements used by legally married straight couples. Instead of providing a "model," then, we will itemize the topics typically addressed in a domestic-partnership contract. Not every topic is likely to be relevant to all domestic partnerships, but the list can serve as a checklist of subjects to be considered.

Property

With property, the general rule is that assets acquired prior to the partnership are retained by the partner who acquired them; assets acquired by one partner through gift or inheritance remain with the recipient; and assets acquired during the partnership may be shared equally or in proportion to each partner's contribution to their acquisition. These general rules may, of course, be modified in any way agreed to by the partners.

In addition, the following issues may require specification:

- Arrangements for ownership and use of co-owned property, or an agreement to keep property separate.
- Division of equity in any co-owned property.
- Management and control of property.
- Value of property improvements, distribution of that value between co-owners, and reimbursement for separate or joint funds used for improvements.
- In the event the partnership dissolves, who keeps the property and who buys out the other partner?
- Terms (or criteria for setting the terms) of a buy-out agreement.

- Division of proceeds from rental property owned by one or both partners.
- Use or division of insurance proceeds if the property is damaged or destroyed.
- Interest in a business venture owned by one or both partners.
- Interest in professional licenses acquired by a partner during the partnership and as a result of the other partner's support—through payment of part or all of the partner's tuition, for example.
- Interest in a partner's retirement pension and other benefits accumulated during the partnership.

Money

- What funds will be held jointly, and what separately?
- Management and use of joint bank accounts.
- Use of individually or jointly owned cash or credit to acquire real or personal property, and how ownership interests relate to each partner's original investments or contributions. (Partners may want to consider preparing a separate agreement to cover large purchases, such as a home or business.)
- Financial or other support during the partnership or in the event of a temporary or permanent break-up.
- Services (other than sexual) provided by each partner during the partnership and reimbursement (if any) for such services.

Health, Medical Care, and Death

- Authority of one partner to make health-care decisions for the other in the event of a partner's incapacity.
- Visitation rights at hospitals and nursing homes.
- Authority to dictate, on behalf of a deceased partner, funeral arrangements and the method of body disposition.
- Partner's rights in a cemetery plot.

Children

- Which partner (if female) will bear children?
- Which rights and responsibilities of child-rearing will be shared?
- What surname will the child use?
- Will the child be adopted by a non-biological parent?
- Child custody and visitation rights in the event of a break-up.
- Obligation for payment of child support during the partnership or in the event of a break-up.
- Authority to make medical and educational decisions on behalf of the child.
- Authority to communicate with school officials regarding the child.
- Guardianship of minor children orphaned by death of a biological parent/partner.

Dispute Resolution

- Agreement to use arbitration or mediation rather than litigation to resolve disputes during the partnership or following a break-up.

- Agreement on a cooling-off period (analogous to a legal separation) before a final termination of the partnership.

Preparing the Contract □

Before drafting a domestic-partnership contract, the partners should discuss at length the intentions and agreements they intend to include in the document. After negotiating the issues detailed above, some couples might wish to retain a lawyer; another option is to rely on one of a variety of self-help books—some of which suggest it is easy to prepare a domestic-partnership contract without legal assistance. Laws governing domestic-partnership contracts vary so widely from state to state, though, that using a one-size-fits-all form can be hazardous.

If substantial assets are involved, we suggest consulting an experienced lawyer to assist with preparation of the contract. In some cases, use of the same lawyer by both parties can create a conflict of interest for the lawyer. Thus, it might be wise for each partner to consult a different lawyer, allowing the lawyers to negotiate a final document. In most cases, though, especially if there is no significant dispute between the partners, use of the same lawyer is acceptable.

Although domestic-partnership contracts are often drafted and signed at the outset of a relationship—or at the outset of the "serious" phase of a relationship, sometimes even to signify the "seriousness" of a relationship—they can be drafted and signed at any stage. Circumstances of individuals and couples often change. Consequently, domestic-partnership contracts are sometimes signed only after the relationship has existed for many months or years.

If neither partner has much in the way of assets and no minor children are involved, a domestic-partnership agreement is probably unnecessary. On the other hand, couples might wish to consider a contract if one partner has substantial assets and the other partner has next to nothing, or if there are (or are about to be) children, or if the partners expect to acquire real estate, or if one partner anticipates acquiring an interest in real estate owned by the other.

□ Are Domestic-Partnership Contracts Enforceable?

In *Marvin v. Marvin* (1976), the leading case involving cohabitation contracts, the California Supreme Court reached three important conclusions: (1) unmarried couples may make binding written contracts; (2) unmarried couples may also make oral contracts; and (3) where no written or oral contract exists, the court may examine the relationship and the conduct of the partners to determine whether an implied contract exists. Since the *Marvin* decision, most state courts faced with the issue of domestic-partnership contracts have enforced written contracts, been divided in cases involving oral contracts, and rejected implied contracts.

An important consideration when drafting a domestic-partnership contract is that it will not be enforced if it states or implies that it was made in consideration of sexual services. Hence, it is crucial that the contract's provisions omit any reference to sex or sexuality; parties to the contract should be identified as "partners" rather than "lovers." In

1981, a California court considered a case in which the services of one partner were described in the contract as "lover, companion, homemaker, traveling companion, housekeeper, and cook." The court held that the sexual services rendered by the complaining partner were the predominant consideration for the contract, which was therefore deemed unenforceable.

Domestic-Partnership Ordinances □

Although valuable in assisting gay and lesbian couples in planning their financial affairs and preparing for the future, domestic-partnership contracts do not provide external validation of gay and lesbian relationships. Thus, they also do not provide a legal framework for dealing with any part of a relationship that goes beyond the contract; for issues not covered by the contract, the law regards gay and lesbian domestic partners as total strangers.

There are, however, a few exceptions to the above rule. In some municipalities domestic-partnership ordinances exist, providing external validation and establishing various rights and responsibilities. For example, the domestic-partnership ordinance adopted by San Francisco in 1991 defines domestic partnership, specifies how it can be terminated, creates obligations between the partners on such matters as sharing the cost of living, and extends full fringe benefits, including health care, to domestic partners of its municipal employees. In the past decade several communities, including Los Angeles, Seattle, Vancouver, Minneapolis, Toronto, and New York, have adopted domestic-part-

nership ordinances. (At the time of this writing, no domestic-partnership laws have been enacted on a statewide
basis.) It should be noted that domestic-partnership ordinances vary widely by municipality.

■ CHILD-RELATED ISSUES

Many gays and lesbians have fathered or borne children in
a previous heterosexual relationship. If so, issues of custody
and visitation are likely to arise. Other issues may arise, depending on local laws, when gay and lesbian couples seek to
become foster or adoptive parents.

Court decisions with respect to custody and visitation are
generally based on "the best interests of the child." Homosexuality is not per se a bar to obtaining or retaining custody
or visitation rights. Nevertheless, homophobic judges have
on many occasions denied custody to homosexuals on the
grounds that the petitioner's partner or the couple's lifestyle
is unsuitable for a minor child. In one case, for example, a
judge denied custody to the child's biological mother on the
grounds that living in a lesbian household would affect the
child's own sexual identity; the court cited no evidence to
support such an outcome.

Another decision involving lesbian coparents denied visitation rights to one partner (a nonbiological, nonadoptive parent) after her 16-year relationship ended, even though the
partners' decision to have children by artificial insemination
was made jointly during the relationship, both women had
acted as parents, and the children regarded both partners as
mothers. The court chose not to expand the definition of par-

ent beyond the biological mother and denied the nonbiological parent/partner custody and visitation rights.

In short, although homosexuality is not grounds for the denial of custody or visitation, there is little doubt it can play a significant role in a court's ultimate decision. A well-crafted domestic-partnership contract can often alleviate such problems. But, until the laws change or homophobia is eliminated, gay and lesbian parents will not be treated the same as their straight counterparts.

Adoption of Children □

Because adoption of children by gays and lesbians is a relatively recent phenomenon, there is little case law on which judges can base their decisions. Hence, the tendency of the courts is to rely on the general rules governing child custody. Consequently, as in custody cases, the court's primary concern when ruling on adoption is the best interests of the child.

Adoption is governed by state statute, and these laws vary to some extent. Florida and New Hampshire expressly prohibit adoption of children by homosexuals. Other states specify that "any adult resident of the state" or "any married or unmarried adult" may adopt children—subject, of course, to what the court deems to be in the best interests of the child. Thus, homophobic judges using "the best interests of the child" criterion may prevent adoption on the grounds that the prospective adopter's homosexual lifestyle would be detrimental to the child's development.

There are two ways of finding a child to adopt: through an

agency or privately. In agency adoptions, the prospective adopter applies to a licensed state or private agency. Since the child's natural parents have already given up their rights to the child, the adoption is sometimes approved immediately by the court, provided a prior investigation of the adopter proved him or her to be satisfactory as a potential parent. In private adoptions, the prospective adopter finds a parent willing to have the child adopted and makes arrangements for the adoption, usually through a lawyer and subject to court approval.

In the adoption investigatory process, it may be possible for the prospective adopter to conceal his or her homosexuality from the court. This is done in an unknown number of cases. It can, however, be hazardous. In one case, an adoption was terminated by the court when the adopter's homosexuality was subsequently discovered.

☐ Adoption by Second Partner

In general, adoption by a nonbiological parent in a domestic partnership is sound practice. It protects the child should the biological parent die, and it reinforces the concept that the domestic partnership is, indeed, a family. Child adoptions by a same-sex partner are usually approved when the biological parent consents to the child's adoption while retaining his or her own parental rights.

■ ADULT ADOPTION

A procedure occasionally used by domestic partners to provide external validation and to establish certain rights and responsibilities is the legal adoption of one adult partner by the other. Many employer-provided benefits, for example, extend to the employee's family, and many rental agreements allow the renter to share the premises with family members but not unrelated individuals. In addition, adult adoption may offer significant tax advantages to the adopting partner.

On the issue of adult adoption, state statutes vary. Arizona and Nebraska expressly prohibit it. In five states—California, Connecticut, Massachusetts, New Jersey, and Nevada—the adopter must be older than the adult adoptee. In New Jersey, the adopter must be at least ten years older than the adoptee, and in Puerto Rico the age difference must be at least 16 years. In the two states that prohibit homosexuals from adopting minors—Florida and New Hampshire—the restriction against homosexuals adopting would seem to apply to the adoption of adults as well. In some other states—Idaho[3] and Virginia,[4] for example—restrictions on adult adoptions are likely to have the practical effect of prohibiting domestic partner adult adoptions.

The legal consequences of gay or lesbian adult adoptions vary from state to state, but in no state does such an adoption confer any power of the adopter over the adoptee. In all states adult adoption automatically disinherits the parents and siblings (but not children) of both the adopter and the adoptee should the adopter die intestate. Parents and siblings of the adopter, and in most cases of the adoptee, have no standing to contest the partner's will, as will contests may be filed only by persons who would gain by invalidating the will.

For most domestic partners, adult adoption might initially seem an attractive solution, but it has significant drawbacks. First and foremost, it is irrevocable. Thus, couples risk finding themselves in the awkward position of being in an adoptive relationship even though their romantic relationship has ended. In such a situation, a former lover who has been adopted may challenge his or her ex-mate's subsequent will even though the relationship has ended. Furthermore, in most states an adoptee loses the right to inherit from his or her natural parents if the natural parents die intestate.

For all these reasons, we do not recommend adult adoption of a domestic partner. The advantages are outweighed by the disadvantages, and most if not all of its benefits can be achieved by means of a domestic-partnership contract, beneficiary designation in a will or a trust, and financial and medical durable powers of attorney.

■ MAKING A DECISION

A domestic-partnership contract addressing rights and responsibilities with respect to the personal, economic, and parenting aspects of a relationship puts partners and their children, if any, in an improved position in many ways. It forces couples to focus on important issues and to govern their lives in terms of their resources and needs in mutually approved ways. The contract enables partners to document themselves as a family unit and to memorialize the extent of their interdependence and commitment. It strengthens the position of each partner should he or she become a party to litigation by providing the court with documentation evidencing the couple's relationship, intentions, and agreements. And, should a break-up occur, the contract—presumably drawn up when emotions were calmer—provides enforceable guidelines concerning the ownership and division of property, provisions for financial support, and the rearing of minor children.

In contrast to legally married straight couples, whose rights and responsibilities are in large part determined by state laws recognizing marriage, gay and lesbian domestic partners must discuss forthrightly many difficult issues and arrive at workable agreements. This is a difficult and emotionally challenging process, requiring a substantial commitment of time and energy, but the result can be a heightened awareness of one another's values and concerns, and a deeper understanding of each partner's strengths and weaknesses.

Notes

[1] In the past several years many municipalities, including Los Angeles, San Francisco, Seattle, Vancouver, Minneapolis, Toronto, and New York, have adopted ordinances providing various degrees of legal status to domestic partnerships.

[2] Although these ordinances vary considerably, they typically establish a procedure for registering the domestic partnership, list employee benefits that accrue to the employee's partner, establish responsibilities of partners to each other, and establish a procedure for terminating the partnership.

[3] Requires the petitioner to be *in loco parentis* with adoptee for over one year while the adoptee is a minor.

[4] Requires the adoptee to be at least 15 years younger than the petitioner.

Chapter 3

YOUR LETTER OF INSTRUCTION

There are other documents besides your will that you may want to prepare now, even though, like your will, they will probably not be needed for quite some time. The letter of instruction and the living will are the two most important of these documents. Although both are recognized in most states as legal documents, they lack the legal force of a will and consequently do not offer complete protection. Nevertheless, gays and lesbians may find these documents provide at least some degree of protection against action from alienated or hostile parents and siblings.

The letter of instruction is an informal document that specifically lists all of your assets and identifies the location of such items as insurance policies, car registration documents, deeds, and other items your survivors will need to settle your estate. Because it is an informal document, it is far easier to revise than your will. And, because it does not become a public document in probate proceedings, you can use it to convey private messages after your death.

The living will is a document that explicitly states your preferences about medical treatment should you become incapacitated or otherwise unable to express yourself when suffering from a terminal illness or injury. Living wills are covered in detail in Chapter 6.

Other documents also offer protection against adverse events. The financial power of attorney names another person who will have the right to handle your financial affairs if you become incapable of making sound decisions. The medical power of attorney does the same for medical treatment. These two documents are also covered in Chapter 6.

THE LETTER OF INSTRUCTION ■

As noted in Chapter 1, wills must be prepared in accordance with legal formalities. Consequently, revising your will each time the nature or value of your possessions changes is likely to be both inconvenient and expensive. For this reason, your will, rather than enumerating everything you own, should dispose of your possessions in general terms. Your will may, of course, bequeath certain possessions—a piece of jewelry, for example—to specific beneficiaries, but it should not specify the disposition of every stock, bond, savings account, motor vehicle, dish, and bauble, because your inventory of these items changes over time.

It is important, however, that you maintain a current record of everything you own so your survivors will not overlook items of value simply because they don't know of their existence or whereabouts. It is all very well to assume that a domestic partner or a close friend is fully aware of your assets and your liabilities—especially if most of your property is owned jointly. If you die simultaneously, however, your survivors will not know what you owned and what you owed unless you have provided them with a current inventory. Leaving such a record, known formally as a letter of instruction, is therefore quite important.

Three further functions can be served by a letter of instruction. First, it can indicate the location of seemingly trivial but very important items—insurance policies, car keys, the key to a safe deposit box, your computer password. Second, it can express your wishes concerning funeral arrangements. (Embodying these wishes in your will assumes it will be read immediately, and often it is not. The letter of instruction can be made more readily accessible than a will, and is more likely to be read shortly after your death.) And, finally, your letter of instruction is the appropriate place for the expression of any private personal wishes or messages to your survivors, since your will, if it requires probate, becomes a public document, available to anyone curious about its contents.

Unlike your will, your letter of instruction is not a legally enforceable document, and its instructions are not binding on your survivors. (As we shall see, your survivors are not always legally bound to honor your funeral preferences, even if specified in your will or letter of instruction.) Despite its name, your letter of instruction merely *informs* your survivors. It cannot instruct them to do anything.

Because it is not a legally enforceable document, your letter of instruction need not follow a particular format. It can take the form of a personal letter, or a number of alternatives that may appeal to you. The appendix includes a modification of a form provided by Citibank. Similar forms are available at stationery stores. People who make frequent changes in their insurance policies or their investments, however, might prefer a loose-leaf binder or a box of index cards.

Whatever form you choose, the location of your letter of instruction should be known to those who are closest to you—your domestic partner, your adult children, a close friend, and perhaps your lawyer. This does not mean that these individuals need or should be given access to it or knowledge of its contents while you are alive. You can, for example, keep it in a locked desk drawer to which only you have the key, in a bank safe deposit box, or in some other private location. Whatever you decide, it should be easily and readily accessible, so you can update it as necessary—every time you buy or sell a stock or open or close a bank account—and so your survivors can find it easily and quickly following your death.

Because it is a highly personal document, it is not possible to specify what the "ideal" letter of instruction should contain. The following list, though, will help you get started. You may not need to include every item, and you may own assets that don't fit into the categories we've listed. Nevertheless, reviewing the list will help make sure you do not overlook anything.

☐ Your Assets

- Bank Accounts, etc.:

    Your letter of instruction need not account for every penny of your net worth, but it should list each bank or credit union account, certificate of deposit, U.S. savings bond, money market account, and any other instrument that represents value. Each year millions of dollars in unclaimed bank accounts revert to state treasuries simply because their original owners or their survivors have lost track of them. Your letter should also include a listing of all other money owed to you—from loans you have made, rents, royalties, land contracts, etc.—and information about the location of documents relating to these items.

- Stocks and Bonds:

    If your stock and bond transactions have involved only one brokerage firm, and if your securities are registered in the broker's street account, your letter of instruction should include (or specify the location of) your most recent statement. If, on the other hand, you use several brokers and the security certificates are in your possession, your letter should include a complete inventory and a schedule of dividend payments, along with information about whether dividend checks are payable to you or automatically deposited in your bank or money-market account.

- Life Insurance Policies:

  Each of your life insurance policies should be inventoried by company, policy number, face value, beneficiary designation, dividend dates, and any loans you have taken against their cash value. The location of the policies should also be specified.

- Medical Benefits:

  If you are covered by a medical plan, your letter of instruction should indicate the coverages and the location of your policy. This is important for your survivors not only for the collection of possible benefits resulting from your terminal illness but for the continuation of any survivor's benefits available to your domestic partner.

- Death Benefits:

  To collect death benefits, your survivors will need your Social Security number, possibly your birth certificate, and evidence of your discharge from military service (if any). Your letter of instruction should provide this information and indicate the location of all relevant documents. It should also specify any union death benefit, or mortgage or credit life insurance that cancels your indebtedness on your death.

- Tangible Property:

  Your letter of instruction should list all of your possessions that involve some sort of registration or title. Real estate, motor vehicles, motor homes, and boats are typical examples. Because your survivors will need the registration documents in order to transfer ownership, their location should be specified. If these items are insured, the letter should indicate the location of each policy and the schedule of premium payments. This is especially important with respect to homeowner's and automobile insurance coverages, because a lapse in premium payments, which can occur all too easily when your survivors are distracted by your death, can leave valuable assets unprotected.

- Funeral and Burial Arrangements:

  If you own a cemetery plot, your letter of instruction should indicate the plot number, the name and location of the cemetery, and the location of the cemetery deed. If you have made advance arrangements with a funeral home, the location of the contract and name of the funeral home should be specified. If you have not made advance arrangements, you may want to express a preference as to type of funeral service, your eulogist, and method of body disposal. Bear in mind, though, that these preferences are not binding on your survivors, and that conflicts sometimes arise between a surviving domestic partner and the deceased's parents or other family members. Unfortunately, such conflicts are difficult to resolve. Furthermore, even if you have made advance arrangements with a funeral home, the arrangement can be overridden by parents willing to sacrifice the payments you have made.

Your Liabilities □

Although a painstaking review of your checkbook can help your survivors identify your recurrent financial obligations, you can ease their task by listing in your letter of instruction all your financial obligations—mortgages, loans, credit-card payments, and installment payments on cars, boats, and major appliances. Your letter should note whether you alone are responsible for the debt or whether someone else, perhaps your domestic partner, cosigned for the loan or credit card. Outstanding debts on cosigned agreements are the responsibility of the surviving cosigner. Debts incurred by you alone, though, will not have to be paid by your survivors if there is insufficient money in your estate to pay them.

Your list of liabilities will also help your survivors determine which of your obligations should be paid promptly in order to avoid foreclosure, repossession, or the termination of services, and which obligations can be delayed until final settlement of your estate.

Your letter of instruction should also list any payments you have made or documents you have signed for goods to be delivered or services to be performed in the future—airline tickets, tour reservations, deposit on a car not yet delivered, taxes paid in advance of their due date in order to gain a tax deduction. Many of these items represent cash that can accrue to your estate if the agreements or reservations are canceled promptly.

☐ Miscellaneous

No matter what your lifestyle, you undoubtedly carry around "in your head" many facts that are not known to your survivors. Thus, your letter of instruction should include any relevant information that you cannot assume your survivors know. The following list is incomplete, but provides examples of the above and may prompt you to think of other items.

- Keys:

    Nothing is more frustrating to survivors than encountering a locked drawer or cabinet for which they can't find the key, or finding a key for which they can't identify the lock. Though you may be able to identify your keys by shape or color, you can't expect your survivors to do the same. Your letter of instruction should specify the location of all important keys and lock combinations—vehicles, safebox, desk drawers, file cabinets, office, safe—and each of these keys should be somehow identified. Keys no longer in use should be discarded.

- Hiding Places:

    Even people who rent bank safeboxes often have secret hiding places at home—to foil burglars or simply to avoid trips to the bank. Your letter of instruction should specify these locations. Of course, if a burglar finds your letter, your hiding place is no longer secure. Since burglars rarely spend time reading personal documents, though, we feel it is better to avoid the far greater risk that your survivors will overlook or be unable to locate some of your highly valued possessions.

- Inconspicuous Valuables:

    The value of most items is apparent at a glance, but not those whose appraisal requires some expertise. Your survivors, especially if they don't share your enthusiasm for or knowledge of such items, may discard as junk highly valuable possessions such as old clocks, china, first-edition books, antiques, artwork, or other items you have painstakingly and lovingly acquired and consider valuable. Thus, your letter of instruction should identify any items that might not otherwise be recognized as valuable or significant and should indicate the approximate value and the location of any documents (bills of sale, receipts, customs declarations) providing evidence of their provenance.

    This listing, if done with care, can serve a second purpose as well. By omitting certain items, it can prevent your survivors from assuming that the omitted items have high value as antiques and taking them, with high hopes, for appraisal by antiques dealers or auctioneers, only to be told that they should be consigned to the local thrift shop.

    Conversely, items having little or no value as an-

tiques may nevertheless have high personal value—
a fourth-generation family Bible or a century-old da-
guerreotype of an ancestor. Sketching the history of
such items in your letter of instruction will not only
increase the items' value in the eyes of your survivors but may also strengthen their feeling for your
family's history.

☐ Your "Letter to the World"

Your letter of instruction also gives you an opportunity to
communicate to one or more of your survivors feelings,
thoughts, or ideas that, for one reason or another, you are unable to express in a face-to-face encounter. You may, for example, want to use your letter to heal a long-standing breach in
a relationship or to explain its origin. You may want to express
affection or respect you are embarrassed to express while
alive. You may want to explain or apologize for actions which,
at one time or another, created problems or raised questions
for your survivors. All of this is especially relevant for individuals alienated from parents, siblings, or adult children.

Although there are no prescriptions or proscriptions as to
your letter of instruction, we recommend that you avoid vin-
dictiveness and that you not express hopes or wishes that
are unlikely to be fulfilled. After all, no purpose is served by
a posthumous revelation that you have resented your brother ever since your parents sent him, but not you, to college,
or by a hope your sister "will see the light" and divorce her
husband. If you want to be remembered fondly, it is wise to
err on the side of tolerance and charity.

Keeping Up to Date ☐

Even if your affairs are complicated, preparing a letter of instruction involves no more than a couple of evenings of concentrated work. The effort will be largely wasted, though, unless you update the letter at regular intervals—at least semiannually if you shift your investments frequently, and in no instance less than annually to account for insurance premiums, automobile changes, and other shifts in your assets and liabilities. We recommend you make updates part of your routine household accounting, especially if you maintain at least part of your letter in the form of a loose-leaf book or set of index cards. You might also find the contents of your letter of instruction useful in budgeting and in calculating your income taxes.

PART TWO
FINANCIAL ISSUES

Chapter 4

HOW TO OWN WHAT YOU HAVE

Anything you own—a bank account, a certificate of deposit, stocks, bonds, real estate, or personal possessions—can be titled in any of several ways when you acquire it. When you buy a car, a home, or shares of stock, the form of your ownership is indicated on your car title, the deed for your home, or your brokerage account. You can also change the form of ownership of property you've had for some time, and on personal possessions, such as your clock collection or your household furnishings, even if you lack documentation proving ownership.

The form of ownership you choose has significant consequences for your control over your property during your life-

time, and even more important consequences when you die.
The form of ownership you choose deserves thoughtful consideration because some forms, once chosen, cannot be
changed without the consent of others.

■ SOLE OWNERSHIP

The simplest form of ownership, sole ownership, has several advantages. To begin with, it gives you complete control
over the property. You can sell the property or use it for
whatever purpose you choose without consulting anyone,

Legal Consequences of Various Forms of Ownership

Form of Ownership	Subject to probate	Subject to federal estate tax	Control during your lifetime
Asset solely owned	Yes	All	Full
Asset owned jointly by spouses	No[1]	One-half	Divided
Asset owned jointly by nonspouses	No[1]	All[3]	Divided
Asset in bank account (Totten) trust	No	All	Full
Asset in custodial account for minors	No	None[4]	Limited
Life insurance owned by insured	No[5]	All	Full
Life insurance owned by other than insured	No[5]	None[6]	None
Life insurance payable to deceased's estate	Yes	All	Full
Asset in a revocable living trust	No	All	Full

1 Provided you are survived by a joint owner.
2 Unless debt was incurred by both joint owners.
3 Except to the extent your estate can prove that a surviving joint owner contributed
to the acquisition or improvement of the asset.
4 Unless you are a custodian as well as a donor.
5 Provided you are survived by a beneficiary designated in the insurance policy.
Otherwise, proceeds become a part of your probate estate.
6 Unless you assigned the policy to another within three years of your death.

---

and you can specify who inherits it after your death. You can set it aside to be used for your child's education or the future purchase of a summer cottage. You can also borrow against it to prepay or refinance a mortgage, to take advantage of an investment or business opportunity, or for any other purpose. In short, sole ownership gives complete control over your assets, providing autonomy, security, freedom, and flexibility.

Nevertheless, sole ownership has several disadvantages. First, it provides no protection against your own impulsive

Bequeathable by will	Subject to creditor's claims before death	Subject to creditor's claims after death	After-death availability to beneficiaries
Yes	Yes	Yes	Delayed
No[1]	Yes	No[2]	Immediate[1]
No[1]	Yes	No[1]	Immediate[1]
No	Yes	No	Immediate
No	No	No	Immediate
No[5]	No	No[5]	Immediate
No	No	No[5]	Immediate
Yes	Yes[7]	Yes	Delayed
No	Yes	No[8]	Immediate[9]

7 Limited to the cash surrender value of the policy.
8 Some states have recently adopted laws permitting creditors, after death, to satisfy their claims from assets left in the deceased's revocable living trust.
9 Subject, however, to all of the terms of the trust, which may include a provision postponing distribution of the asset.

behavior. A joint owner might offer a second opinion that could save you from losing your assets in an ill-fated business venture.

Conversely, if an exceptional opportunity for investment suddenly arises at a time when you are away from home or incapacitated, a joint owner could act on your behalf. This function can also be served by anyone to whom you grant a financial power of attorney. (See Chapter 6).

Furthermore, as long as you have sole ownership of your property, you retain full responsibility for paying local, state, and federal income taxes on whatever it earns. And whatever you own will be subject to the claims of your creditors, not only during your lifetime but also after your death. Perhaps more importantly, all assets you hold as sole owner will, on your death, be subject to probate administration and possibly to the federal gift and estate tax. Hence, you may want to consider the alternative forms of ownership discussed below.

■ JOINT TENANCY WITH RIGHTS OF SURVIVORSHIP

Despite the attractions of sole ownership, its disadvantages prompt many people to choose an alternative. A popular choice is joint tenancy with rights of survivorship, usually abbreviated on bank and brokerage accounts as "JTWROS." This form of joint ownership can be established with one or more other persons—domestic partner, parent, sibling, friend, child—and is available for any kind of property—bank and brokerage accounts, real estate, motor vehicles, and even personal belongings.

The most significant aspect of joint ownership is that on the death of one owner the asset passes automatically to the surviving owner or owners without the need for probate. This is why joint ownership has been called "the poor man's will." On the other hand, neither joint owner can bequeath the jointly owned property through his or her will, since its disposition to the surviving owner is predetermined. An additional advantage is that upon the death of one joint owner the deceased's creditors have no claim on any part of the property because it belongs to the surviving joint owner(s) rather than the deceased's estate.

Some gay and lesbian domestic partners establish joint tenancy for some or all of their assets as a symbol of their love and their desire to share their possessions. If the relationship unravels, however, serious problems arise. First, in many types of joint tenancy—bank and brokerage accounts, for example—either partner can withdraw or otherwise take control of the entire jointly held property. Hence, there is the danger that the departing partner may abscond with those jointly held assets. This danger can be avoided if the terms of the joint tenancy specify that two signatures are required for any withdrawal, but such a provision detracts from the often symbolic value of the joint tenancy.

A joint tenancy can be dissolved by mutual agreement of the owners, but this is unlikely when the owners part on bad terms. When legally married straight couples divorce, courts routinely dissolve joint tenancies as part of the divorce settlement. But gay and lesbian domestic partners have no such option, since dissolution of their partnership is not subject to the aegis of divorce proceedings. Thus, joint tenancy with a domestic partner should be used only when the relationship is extremely stable.

Gay and lesbian domestic partners seeking to place assets into joint ownership face an additional handicap not encountered by legally married couples. Because gifts between spouses are unlimited and untaxable, a bank account, a stock portfolio, or a home can be titled in joint tenancy even though it was acquired by only one member of a married couple. For gay and lesbian couples, though, unless each joint owner can show he or she contributed to the assets placed in joint ownership, half the assets will be regarded as a gift. And lifetime gifts in excess of $10,000 are subject to the federal gift tax

This obstacle can be overcome, though—at least with respect to bank accounts, certificates of deposit, and mutual funds—because the gift does not take effect (the assets do not become a gift) until the noncontributing joint tenant withdraws money for his or her own use. If these withdrawals do not exceed $10,000 annually, no tax liability is incurred.

Joint ownership costs little or nothing to establish. For bank or brokerage accounts, it involves nothing more than establishing (or changing) the registration of the account. Real estate can be transferred into joint ownership by preparing and signing a new deed. And personal property requires only documentary proof (such as a bill of sale) that the item was purchased jointly or, lacking such proof, a written statement to the effect that the property is jointly owned.

PAY-ON-DEATH ACCOUNTS ■

A useful compromise between sole and joint ownership is what is known as a "pay-on-death" bank account. Under this arrangement, the person who establishes the account retains sole control of the account balance but specifies on the account that upon his or her death the balance will pass automatically to the person(s) named on the account as the beneficiary.

This type of account embodies the advantages (and some of the disadvantages) of sole ownership and probate avoidance, but its greatest advantage is that the beneficiary can be changed at any time or eliminated entirely. Whereas a joint bank account may be difficult to unwind, the pay-on-death account can be changed by simply revising the title of the account. This provides an escape for one domestic partner in the event the partnership terminates.

In Arkansas, Colorado, Kansas, Michigan, Minnesota, Missouri, Montana, Nebraska, New Mexico, North Dakota, Ohio, Oregon, Virginia, Washington, West Virginia, Wisconsin, and Wyoming, a transfer-on-death designation can be used for stocks and bonds. Any broker can provide you with forms to designate a beneficiary for your individual securities or brokerage account.

TOTTEN TRUST ■

Another way to provide assets to a child beneficiary is to set up a Totten trust bank account, also known as a discretionary trust account. This trust is recognized in most states, and is likely to be available at your local bank. Setting up a

Totten trust involves nothing more than filling out a signature card designating you as the trustee and naming one or more beneficiaries.

On your death, the account balance passes to the named beneficiaries without probate. Until then you can add to the account or withdraw from it for any purpose. The beneficiaries have no access until your death. The one disadvantage of the Totten trust is that it is restricted to investments offered by a bank—savings accounts and certificates of deposit—which may not offer the most favorable returns.

■ THE REVOCABLE LIVING TRUST

A revocable living trust is a legal entity into which you can transfer assets in any amount and of any kind. It is one of the most flexible arrangements for holding your assets. Although originally used only by the very rich, revocable living trusts are becoming more widely utilized as increasing numbers of middle-income people recognize its many significant advantages.

The revocable living trust, which embodies many of the functions of a will, has two very important features. First, you can appoint yourself as trustee. Thus, you can retain full control of the trust property during your lifetime, including the right to sell it, add to it, or otherwise dispose of it. You can also specify the terms under which distribution of the trust property can be made during your lifetime or after your death. You can, for example, specify that no beneficiary shall receive his or her share before reaching age 30, or that the share of one of them must be used in whole or in part for college tuition. In this respect a trust is far more flexible than a will. In addition, the terms of the trust agreement may be easily modified at any time.

The second important feature is that trust assets, because they belong to the trust rather than you, are not subject to probate when you die. Thus, on your death, the assets are, in most states, generally not available to pay your debts. Upon your incapacity or death, management of the trust is taken over by a successor trustee appointed by you when you establish or amend the trust. Successor trustees are obligated to manage and distribute the trust's assets according to the terms of the trust agreement.

For gay or lesbian domestic partners, the great advantage of a revocable living trust over joint tenancy is that it allows the person who establishes and funds the trust to name his or her partner as beneficiary of the trust income, principal, or both, while still retaining full control of the trust assets during his or her life. Thus, if the relationship begins to crumble, the partner who established the trust, if he or she wishes, can amend the agreement to deprive the beneficiary partner of further benefits. Similarly, you can protect the interests of your children by naming them as beneficiaries of the trust. These same strategies can be utilized by legally married spouses, but their trust assets are available as part of a divorce settlement, whereas those of domestic partners are not.

Although revocable living trusts are effective in avoiding probate administration of your estate, they typically offer no advantage with respect to taxes. Because you control the trust's assets and the use of their earnings, you remain liable for all income taxes. You do not pay gift tax on assets you transfer to the trust, but all trust assets are included as part of your estate for federal estate tax purposes. And the beneficiaries of the trust normally must pay any state inheritance taxes.

The trust agreement is not a simple document. In addition to naming the trustee and the successor trustee, it spells out in detail what each of them can and cannot do, and how long the trust is to remain in existence. It specifies who the beneficiaries are, and when, how, and under what conditions they are to receive their share of the trust assets.

Any beneficiary may at any time file a lawsuit charging the trustee with violating the terms of the trust. Thus, we don't recommend you draft your trust agreement without professional assistance. You may be tempted to use one of the ready-made, fill-in-the-blanks trust forms available in various self-help books, but a trust is a highly personal document that must be coordinated with a will. No ready-made form can take into account all the special details your trust agreement must include.

Another option is to rely on one of the growing number of firms which, taking advantage of the growing popularity of living trusts, market trust-preparation services through telemarketing and/or invitations to seminars. Many of these firms have been accused of overcharging, neglecting to properly transfer all their clients' assets into the trust, and urging clients to shift assets into financial investments on which the company earns a commission.

If you wish to establish a revocable living trust, we recommend you hire a lawyer to prepare your trust agreement, preferably one experienced in estate planning—not necessarily your regular lawyer. If you live in or near a large city, you will probably be able to find an estate-planning lawyer with a reputation for being knowledgable about and sensitive to the concerns of gays and lesbians.

CUSTODIAL ACCOUNT FOR MINORS ■

If a portion of your assets is intended for the college education of a child, you may want to consider establishing a custodial account for minors. Under this arrangement, which is available in every state and can be used for many types of investments, assets are registered as "[Your name as custodian] [the minor's name] under the Uniform Gifts to Minors Act." A separate account must be established for each minor you intend to benefit. There is no requirement that you serve as the custodian. You can, if you prefer, nominate as custodian your domestic partner, a sibling, a parent, or a friend.

Under the federal gift and estate tax law you can contribute to the custodial account a maximum of $10,000 a year without incurring any gift tax. And anyone else—your parents or your partner, for example—can contribute the same annual tax-free amount.

Assets in a custodial account you have established are not subject to probate on your death, even if you are the custodian, because the assets belong to the child and not you.

Taxes on the earnings of a custodial account are the liability of the child, not the custodian. Until age 14, on annual income over $1,400, the child pays federal income tax at the parent's rate. But once past this age, the child pays at his or her own rate, which is likely to be lower than that of the parent.

Assets placed in a custodial account may not be used for ordinary parental obligations such as food or clothing for the child. They may, however, be used by the custodian for extraordinary expenses such as summer camp, music lessons, or orthodontia.

The major disadvantage of the custodial account is that ownership of all its assets is automatically transferred to the child when he or she reaches the age of majority. Thus, there is nothing you can do about it if the child decides to use the assets to buy a sports car rather than to pay college tuition.

■ TRUST FOR MINORS

Another form used to accumulate assets for a child is the trust for minors, also known as a Section 503(c) trust (in reference to the section of the Internal Revenue Code that authorizes it). A 503(c) trust has several advantages over a custodial account. First, it withholds the assets from the minor until age 21 (or beyond) rather than age 18. It also allows the trustee—either you or a person you designate—to specify at what intervals, in what amounts, and for what purposes assets are to be distributed to the child. In addition, if you establish separate funds within the trust, it can include as beneficiaries several minors rather than only one, and the trust can continue beyond the beneficiaries' age of majority if they feel it is being managed productively. (If the beneficiaries do not agree to an extension of the distribution date, the trust terminates when they reach the age of 21.) Lastly, it can include real estate in addition to all other types of assets.

The tax advantages of a trust for minors are fewer than those of a custodial account. The minors pay taxes on whatever income they receive from the trust. The trust pays taxes on all other income.

MAKING A CHOICE ■

There is no need to choose one form of ownership to the exclusion of all others. You may well decide to keep some of your assets in sole ownership, some in joint tenancy, some in a Totten trust account and others in a revocable living trust, shifting from one form to another as your personal circumstances change.

Chapter 5

WHAT SHAPE IS YOUR NEST EGG?

In this chapter we offer a review of various investment options, along with an examination of the pitfalls associated with some of those options. There is today a large array of possibilities for investing money, and careful planning can help maximize your return on both short-term and long-term investments.

Every investor allocates some assets to satisfy short-term needs—a rainy-day fund in case of unemployment or temporary disability, for example—and other assets for long-term needs—a down payment for a home, for example, or college tuition for a young child.

Assets needed to meet short-term needs should be invested so they can be liquidated quickly, at no cost, and with little or no loss in value. Easy liquidity, as we shall see, inevitably leads to a relatively low rate of return.

Assets designated for long-term needs, however, can be put into investments that may not be easily or quickly liquidated, that incur transaction costs in liquidation, and that fluctuate significantly in value so that they may be worth considerably more (or less) when liquidated than when purchased. Long-term investments generally produce a higher rate of return than short-term investments.

INVESTMENT RISKS ∎

It is important to recognize that no investment, even an investment in U.S. Treasury bonds backed by "the full faith and credit of the United States," is completely safe. Every investment is subject to one or more of the following risks.

Inflation □

The rate of inflation affects all investments. If, for example, the interest rate on a savings account is 3 percent and the current rate of inflation is 3.2 percent, you lose purchasing power on every dollar invested even before you pay income tax on the interest income.

Credit Risk □

If you buy stocks or bonds, for example, there is always the possibility that the issuer will go bankrupt or encounter financial difficulties that reduce or destroy the value of your investment. Many people believe the best predictor of future return is recent past behavior. Those individuals tend to limit their investments to "blue-chip" securities such as IBM or AT&T. But even blue-chip securities can decline in value. Further, dividends from blue-chip corporations tend to be lower than those of less prominent corporations.

☐ Liquidity

Whether you can sell a security for as much as you paid for it is a question that applies to many kinds of securities, but it affects some kinds more dramatically than others. To begin with, some investments—most notably certificates of deposit—impose a penalty for early withdrawal. Other securities may be so lightly traded that you may have to wait weeks to find a buyer.

■ WHERE TO GET ADVICE

Novice investors seeking advice will find no shortage of it. It comes from several sources, but none of them can demonstrate a consistent record of success. To begin with, a variety of books, whose titles vary only in their degree of hype, promise readers success in the stock market. But if one considers the labor involved in writing and publishing a book, one might conclude that, if the advice contained therein were sound, the author would gain more for less labor by following his or her own advice than by producing a get-rich-quick book.

In addition, many people call themselves professional financial planners. Some charge a flat fee for a one-time session. Others follow your investments periodically, taking as their fee a percentage of the total value of your investments. Still others charge a consulting fee and a commission for acquiring for you the investments they recommend. No financial planner has an untarnished record, and none offers reimbursement for losses resulting from their advice.

Full-service brokers give "free" advice if you put your investments in their hands, though you still pay for this advice in the form of higher commissions than those charged by discount brokers (who offer no advice whatsoever).

The biggest problem with advice from a broker is that it represents a clear conflict of interest. On one hand, you expect impartial advice. On the other, brokers earn a commission every time they buy or sell anything for or from your account. Hence, you can never know whether a broker's recommendation to buy or sell is aimed at improving your account or generating commissions. Frequent buying and selling by a broker leading to high commissions with no discernible improvement in the total value of an investment portfolio is known as "churning." The fact that there is a name for this phenomenon should be enough to alert investors that they should, at least, keep an eye on investments handled by a full-service broker.

Another problem with full-service brokers stems from the fact that the most important element of successful investing is the timely acquisition of information—the anticipated merger of two corporations, for example. When a brokerage firm acquires information, it is learned by or immediately funneled to senior brokers, who typically offer it to their largest clients first. If you have a smaller account handled by a junior broker, the information is likely to have little or no value by the time it trickles down to him or her, since the price of a stock typically rises after its recommendation by a large brokerage firm, negating your opportunity to "buy low."

It is nearly impossible to evaluate investment advice. Some financial analysts suggest the best way to pick stocks is to pin your newspaper's financial pages to the wall, toss a few darts, and buy whatever stocks you hit.

All of this may lead you to choose a "discount" broker. Discount brokers offer no advice; they merely execute orders you give to buy or sell. The word "discount," however, is rather elastic; commissions for buying or selling 100 shares of stock can range from more than $75 to as little as $9 depending on the broker. A review of ads in financial journals and major newspapers can give you information on commission rates and other details.

■ YOUR GOALS

In making an investment, some people are mainly interested in maximizing the yield—the cash returned in the form of interest or dividends. Others are primarily concerned with appreciation—an increase in the value of the stocks or bonds they hold. If you need current income from your investments, you will probably focus on yield. If you don't need immediate income and you are concerned about your income-tax bracket, you may prefer appreciation, because when you sell an appreciated asset the capital gains tax is as low as 20 percent, no matter how high your tax bracket. Of course, you don't realize the appreciation until you sell your investment, and once you have done so your appreciation comes to an end, whereas interest or dividends continue for as long as you own the investment.

Some mutual funds advertise neither their yield nor their appreciation, but combine both in a significantly higher figure that they call total return. The problem with this is that you can't be sure how much of this figure represents yield and how much represents appreciation. To make an informed judgment, you need to know rates for both yield and appreciation.

CHOICES ■

Despite the risks, investing is generally far superior to keeping your spare cash under your mattress or in a passbook savings account. What follows is a list of investment options, ranging in risk from low to high. Most financial advisers suggest a variety of investments. If one investment goes bad, perhaps the others will do well. A generally accepted tenet of investing is that diversification minimizes the potential for disaster.

Bank and Credit Union Accounts □

In today's world, a checking account is a virtual necessity. Despite the recent flurry of bank mergers, competition among banks is still considerable. Shopping around for the best terms is well worth your while. Most banks offer a variety of checking accounts, the fees for which depend largely on the minimum balance you are willing to maintain. The account you choose will depend largely on your checking activity, but generally you would do well to choose an account that requires the lowest minimum balance. Then you can invest other assets elsewhere.

A savings account is virtually worthless, since you can get a much better interest rate and virtually the same flexibility from a money market account, described later in this chapter.

□ Certificates of Deposit

Certificates of deposit, offered by banks and credit unions in various denominations for various periods of time, pay a fixed rate of interest for their duration and then return the face amount to you for reinvestment. The longer the duration of the certificate, the higher the interest it pays.

Because banks and credit unions are federally insured up to $100,000, credit risk on certificates of deposit is nonexistent. Liquidity risk, however, is considerable because a substantial penalty is imposed on withdrawals made before expiration of the certificate's term. Interest risk is also significant, especially if the term of the certificate is long. If you have $10,000 to invest in certificates of deposit, the sensible approach is to invest only $1,000 initially, and then another $1,000 every six months. Doing this protects most of your money from a rise in the interest rate.

□ Money Market Mutual Funds

A wiser investment than certificates of deposit is the money market mutual fund, offered by scores of investment companies. Although these funds are not insured by the government, their credit risk is low. In the more than 20 years they have existed, no money market mutual fund has defaulted. Their interest risk is also low because the rate they pay varies from day to day, reflecting fluctuations in the prime rate, and interest is credited to your account daily. The rate money market mutual funds pay is almost always higher than the rate banks pay on certificates of deposit.

The value of each money market mutual fund share remains constant at one dollar. You can add to your account at any time, usually in minimum amounts of $50. The liquidity risk is nonexistent because you can withdraw money, usually in minimum amounts of $250 or $500, at any time by writing a draft—essentially the same as a check. In addition, there are municipal money market funds that are exempt from federal and sometimes state income taxes.

Money market mutual funds vary somewhat in the interest they pay. Their current performance is listed periodically in financial journals and major newspapers. In general, money market mutual funds are more rewarding and more flexible than certificates of deposit.

Stock and Bond Mutual Funds □

A key to successful investing is diversification into several stocks or bonds, but diversification is almost impossible for the many individuals whose income does not permit them to buy, say, 100 shares of stock or a $5,000 bond in half a dozen different corporations. To overcome this obstacle, mutual funds buy thousands of shares in scores of companies and offer their own shares to individual investors, thus permitting the small investor to achieve diversification.

The many thousands of available mutual funds differ wide-ly in their costs and focus. Many impose on the investor a "load"—a charge of 2 to 4.5 percent, sometimes even more, deducted from each investment. And some impose on in-vestors a 12B charge, used by the mutual fund to pay for its promotional activities. This charge is deducted from your balance annually. In addition, some funds charge your ac-count for each withdrawal.

If you buy a "no load" fund, your total investment goes to the purchase of shares at what is called the "net asset value," and when you sell shares you receive cash representing the net asset value on the day you sell. Most financial experts agree that "load" funds generally do not perform any better than "no load" funds.

The focus of mutual funds varies widely. Some specialize in foreign companies. "Sector" funds, as the name implies, restrict their investment to companies in specific market sectors—utilities or pharmaceuticals, for example. Some funds emphasize growth, others income, and still others a combination of both. Some invest only in bonds or only in stocks, whereas others invest in both. Some mutual funds re-strict their investments to bonds exempt from federal and in some cases state income taxes. Because of this wide variety, some investors diversify their investment portfolio by buying shares of several funds.

Mutual fund prices change daily, depending on price changes in their underlying securities. Their daily prices are available in financial journals and major newspapers, and their historical performance can be found in *Standard and Poor's Stock Guide*, available in many public libraries.

Bonds □

A bond, whether it is issued by a corporation or a unit of government, is essentially a promissory note. The issuer promises to pay the investor a stated rate of interest during the bond's lifetime—anywhere from two to 30 years—and to repay you the bond's face value at the end of its term. The interest rate depends on the financial stability of the issuer and the life span of the bond. Reflecting the credit risk, well-established corporations will pay a lower rate than corporations whose future is uncertain. And reflecting the interest risk, bonds with a shorter maturity pay a lower rate than those with a longer maturity.

Bonds issued by state and local governments are generally tax-free, and are available in two types. "General obligation" bonds represent an obligation of the government unit that issues them—the city, county, or state, for example. "Revenue" bonds depend for the payment of interest, not on the governmental unit that issues them, but on the earnings of a specific unit—a toll bridge, for example. Obviously, general obligation bonds are safer than revenue bonds.

The prospect of earning bond interest not subject to income tax may be very tempting, but the savings you anticipate may be illusory, as taxable bonds usually yield a higher rate. You can determine whether a tax-free bond offers an advantage by applying this simple formula:

Interest rate of the bond divided by (1 - your tax bracket)

Thus, if you are in the 28% tax bracket and are considering a tax-free bond paying 6%, the formula

$$6 \text{ divided by } (1 - .28) = 8.33$$

would tell you that the 6% bond is not the best option if you can find a taxable bond yielding more than 8.33%.

Bonds are generally a safe investment, and most pay a higher rate of interest than you can earn through other sources. Provided that the issuer remains in good financial health, the credit risk is low. The liquidity risk is also low because if you need your investment before the bond matures, you can usually sell the bond through a broker in what is called the secondary market. Similarly, you can shorten a bond's maturity period by purchasing on the secondary market bonds that were issued some time ago.

The inflation risk, however, is considerable. If, for example, you pay $10,000 for a 20-year bond that pays 6.5% interest annually, at the end of 20 years you will get back your $10,000, but inflation is certain to have diminished its purchasing power. And during the lifetime of your bond, whenever interest rates rise, the value of your bond drops in the secondary market because the 6.5% interest rate becomes less attractive to a potential buyer.

But if interest rates drop, won't the 6.5% rate become more attractive and thus raise the value of your bond? Possibly, but not necessarily. Many bonds are "callable"—the issuer retains the right to call in the bond after a certain time peri-od, and to give you back its face value or a specified price that is slightly higher than face value. Bond issuers will call in bonds if they see the lower-interest environment as an op-portunity to issue a new series of bonds paying a lower in-terest rate.

If bonds strike you as an attractive investment, you will do better to choose general-obligation bonds that are not callable and have a relatively short term. Bonds can be bought and sold through any broker, and the transaction cost is relatively low.

Stocks □

Although the stock market tends to fluctuate—sometimes wildly—most financial analysts agree that over the long term an investment in common stocks is superior to other invest-ments. Hence, even if you own shares in one or more mutu-al funds, you may also want to invest directly in individual stocks, especially for the long term.

In choosing a stock, you should focus on one of two goals—yield (dividends) or share appreciation—since the two goals tend to be mutually exclusive. Public utilities, for example, tend to pay good dividends, but their price per share tends to remain stable. High-tech stocks, on the other hand, often pay no dividends but hold the promise of a sub-stantial rise in share value.

Transaction costs for buying and selling individual stocks are also a consideration. If, for example, you buy 100 shares of a stock at $10 per share and your commission is $50, the share price will have to rise by 5 percent before you break even.

Nevertheless, there is some satisfaction to be gained from individual stock ownership. Dividends and annual reports come directly to you, and there is something to be said for the feeling of participation in the directions and goals of a corporation, even though such participation is largely illusory.

The greatest danger in owning stock directly involves predicting whether the market will, in the future, rise or fall. No-one, not even the most experienced manager of stock mutual funds, can make totally accurate predictions. For most investors, then, the rule of "buy and hold" makes sense since most stocks tend to rise over long periods. Some analysts, though, discourage falling in love with a particular stock, and suggest selling when it has appreciated by 30 percent.

An advantage of direct ownership of stock is participation in dividend reinvestment programs offered by many corporations. Under these plans, your periodic dividends, instead of being paid to you, are used to buy additional shares at the then-current price—with no brokerage fees. In addition, many corporations permit additional cash payments for this cost-free investment. Such programs can, over the years, substantially increase your initial investment.

☐ Options, Commodities, Futures

Proponents of the stock market like to create the impression that in buying stock you are investing in America's industrial productivity. This is true on the rare occasions when investors buy an initial offering of stock issued by a fledgling corporation in need of capital for rapid expansion. But the overwhelming majority of stock trades have nothing to do with the issuing company. They are little more than bets, with the buyer betting the stock price will rise and the seller betting it will fall.

Does this kind of betting differ from what goes on in Las Vegas? In some respects it does. To begin with, gambling on stocks does not depend entirely on chance. Careful research and study can help you increase your gains and reduce your losses. Moreover, although you may suffer losses, your wager on stocks is unlikely to be wiped out completely.

Certain kinds of stock-market transactions are far more dependent on luck than others. At the top of the list are investments in commodities, futures, and options. Simply put, it is impossible to predict accurately whether the price of wheat (or any commodity) will rise or fall, since the price of wheat is dependent almost entirely on supply, which is dependent almost entirely on the weather, which is totally unpredictable. Thus, an investment in "commodity futures" depends as much on luck as a game of blackjack or craps at the local casino.

The same generally holds true of options to buy or sell a certain stock in the future—a strategy that holds out the promise of substantial gains in return for a small investment. Again, you have no way of accurately predicting whether the stock will go up or down. If you guess correctly you stand to make money, perhaps a considerable amount, by buying or selling at the right time. If you guess incorrectly, you lose the money you paid for the option.

One kind of option can occasionally be useful. If, for example, you own a stock that is now selling at $34 and you are willing to sell it at $35, you may be able to sell a "covered call." Selling the call obligates you to sell the stock to the purchaser of the call at $35 during the life of the call. If the stock price rises beyond $35, you still must sell at $35. In addition to the sale price, though, you keep the money you earned from selling the call. If the price does not reach $35 before the call expires, you keep both the call price and the stock. Covered calls should be sold cautiously because the buyer of the call may know more than you do. But they can give you some additional income if you are clearly willing to sell the stock at $35.

Just as you would not take a substantial part of your money to Atlantic City or Las Vegas in the hope of tripling it in an afternoon, the same thinking should keep you from putting a large portion of your assets into these speculative investments.

PART THREE

ISSUES OF ILLNESS AND MORTALITY

Chapter 6

ANTICIPATING DISABILITY

Although no-one expects to become seriously injured or critically ill, each of us is likely, if we live long enough, to become incapacitated to some extent before dying. Physical incapacity through injury or illness can occur at any time. Mental incapacity generally occurs later in life, although it too can occur at any time. Both possibilities require advance planning, because planning is impossible once the incapacity has occurred. In this chapter we discuss the appointment of a surrogate to handle financial and health-care decisions if and when you are no longer able, as well as alternatives for paying for long-term health care.

■ MANAGING YOUR FINANCES DURING DISABILITY

If and when you become incapacitated you will need someone who can act on your behalf in handling your financial affairs—bank deposits and withdrawals, bill paying, check cashing, investment management, the buying and selling of property, and other transactions. The various techniques discussed below allow you to name a person who will take responsibility for your assets should the need arise. It is important to note that preparations must generally be completed before the onset of your incapacity. Most of the procedures, although widely used, have significant limitations. Nevertheless, each offers a degree of comfort and protection. For gays and lesbians, the element of protection—from hostile family, hospital and bank administrators, and others—is especially important.

□ Guardianships and Conservatorships

When a person is already incapacitated, a guardian can be appointed to manage his or her personal affairs. If the assets are substantial, a conservator can be appointed for purposes of financial management. Such appointments can be made only by petition to a court, usually the probate court. The petitioner—your domestic partner, a relative, a close friend—must file a petition with the court for the appointment. In most cases a lawyer must be retained and compensated to see the process through to completion. If the person for whom the guardianship is sought objects to the appointment, he or she may contest it, usually with the assistance of yet another lawyer. The court may also require the testimony of a physician, who must also be compensated, to establish the patient's lack of competence. The process can be expensive and time-consuming, and if the allegedly incapacitated person contests the appointment, emotionally devastating for everyone involved.

Once a guardianship or conservatorship has been established, it is subject to continuous supervision by the probate court. Guardians are required to report any major decisions relating to the welfare of the person under their supervision, and conservators must report every transaction carried out on behalf of the person whose assets and affairs they are managing.

Although there may be good reason for this supervision by the court, most people find the entire arrangement bothersome and expensive. More importantly, a person under a guardianship or conservatorship automatically surrenders to the guardian or the conservator most of his fundamental rights.

Representative Payeeships □

Several states have established a procedure for the management of money known as "representative payeeship," to be used in connection with state and federal benefits programs. The appointed representative can be a spouse or a child of the recipient, but not a domestic partner. The representative receives and manages the money on the recipient's behalf, applying it to the cost of support and health care, and investing any balance.

Representative payeeships are attractive because, compared to conservatorships, they are relatively easy to establish. The government agency making the payment determines whether the representative payeeship should be created, avoiding the need to apply to the probate court. On the other hand, the representative payeeship is limited in scope, since it applies to one benefit only. Thus, it is useful when the beneficiary is relying entirely on veterans' benefits or Social Security, but not if the beneficiary has several sources of nongovernmental income. It also does not allow a gay or lesbian (or straight) domestic partner to serve as the appointed representative.

☐ Shared Ownership

Some people concerned with the possibility of future incapacity convert their solely owned property into shared ownership with a domestic partner, family member, or other person. A bank account, a brokerage account, or even a home can be transferred into joint ownership for its management when disability occurs. But joint ownership of assets is difficult to unwind and has several limitations, detailed in Chapter 4. In general, shared ownership is not a desirable option if its major purpose is merely to have someone act on your behalf in the event of disability.

☐ Revocable Living Trust

The revocable living trust, also described in Chapter 4, is especially useful in cases of incapacity because the trustee can immediately manage, invest, and reinvest trust assets without prior court approval or intervention. However, the incapacitated person must have established and funded the trust before the onset of incapacity. Finding a suitable trustee may also be a problem, and if the assets are modest, the expense and bother of establishing and maintaining a trust may not be worthwhile.

Financial Power of Attorney □

A more useful and flexible alternative, the financial power of attorney, has none of the limitations of guardianships, conservatorships, representative payeeships, shared ownership, or revocable living trusts. In this context, the word "attorney" is a misnomer, since the empowered person can be any adult—a domestic partner, a relative, a close friend, or even a bank—and need not be (and rarely is) an attorney. Hence, in the discussion that follows, we will refer to the "attorney" as the "agent."

Once executed by you—the "principal"—the power of attorney document authorizes your designated agent to take virtually any action with respect to financial and property management on your behalf except the signing and revocation of your will.

Obviously, then, your choice of an agent is critical. The person selected must be trustworthy and have good business sense, and should be available and willing to serve over what may be an extended period of time. The agent, unless it is a bank, serves without compensation. For this reason a domestic partner, a family member, or any potential beneficiary of your estate may be a good choice. You should also designate a successor agent in case your first choice is unavailable or unwilling to serve when the need arises. It is possible to select two persons to act as co-agents, but doing so can lead to problems if the two individuals cannot agree on a particular course of action.

One advantage of the power of attorney is that, unlike a guardianship or a conservatorship, it does not require court approval or supervision. A power of attorney also leaves you with a greater degree of control. You choose your own agent and specify when and in what circumstances the agent can act. You can revoke the power of attorney document at any time. And while the power of attorney is in force, you can handle your financial affairs however you like for as long as you remain competent.

Unlike joint ownership, power of attorney retains for you exclusive ownership and control of your assets. And, unlike a revocable living trust, there is no need to change title on your assets. Moreover, power of attorney forms (see Appendix) are available at most office-supply stores and can be prepared without the assistance of a lawyer. A power of attorney document can be executed by any adult who is mentally competent and free of duress or undue influence. It represents a private agreement between you and your appointed agent and need not be filed with a court or otherwise made public.

□ Durable Power of Attorney

Until recently the power of attorney was revoked automatically when you became incompetent. Today, however, all states recognize what is called a durable power of attorney, which survives incompetency and is not revoked until you sign a revocation or die.

Limited Power of Attorney □

The limited of power of attorney restricts the agent's authority to a specific activity—the sale of a house, for example, or the management of a checking account. Limited powers of attorney are useful even in the absence of incapacity—when, for example, you are out of the country. The limited power of attorney is durable in that it survives incompetency and at the same time temporary in that it expires when the specified transactions have been completed.

General Power of Attorney □

The general power of attorney gives your agent the right to handle all your financial affairs and is available in two forms, the present power of attorney, and the future power of attorney. The present power of attorney takes effect as soon as the power of attorney document is executed and is useful for anyone who needs immediate management of his or her financial affairs. The future power of attorney, on the other hand, goes into effect only after the principal becomes incapacitated. Because the future power of attorney gives the agent no immediate power, the power of attorney document should specify that the principal's incapacity is to be determined by a specified physician. You will probably want to select your attending physician. Once a physician certifies you can no longer manage your financial affairs, the power of attorney takes effect.

Acceptability of the Power of Attorney □

A power of attorney is useless unless the bank, insurance company, brokerage firm, or any other third party is willing to accept and act upon it. Acceptance of a present power of attorney is likely to be routine if photocopies of the document are distributed to the parties involved and if the document contains a clause exempting these institutions from any liability they might incur by relying on it. It should also contain a statement that photocopies are valid, although some third parties will recognize only the original. In addition, it should be witnessed and, if real estate is involved, notarized and recorded with the register of deeds.

In the case of a future power of attorney, copies should not be distributed except to your personal physician who, when the time comes, will append a statement certifying your incapacity. In all cases, your agent should receive a photocopy and be informed about the location of the original.

☐ Revoking a Power of Attorney

A power of attorney, because it is a voluntary arrangement, can be revoked by the principal at any time prior to incapacity. Revocation requires nothing more than the execution of a form called "Revocation of Power of Attorney" (see Appendix), which need not be witnessed. If the original power of attorney was recorded with the register of deeds, however, a witnessed and notarized revocation should also be recorded.

Copies of the revocation should be submitted promptly (by certified mail, if necessary) to the agent and to any third parties who honored the original appointment. The original document should be retained with your records. If you revoke the power of attorney in order to appoint a new agent, the new power of attorney should contain a clause reciting that the previous power of attorney has been revoked and that the current version is effective immediately.

Mental competence, just as it is required to execute a power of attorney, is required to revoke a power of attorney. If the principal becomes incompetent, subsequent revocation requires an interested person to petition the probate court for the appointment of a conservator, who may then execute a revocation on behalf of the principal.

Terminating a Power of Attorney □

Aside from revocation, there are several ways in which a power of attorney can terminate. A power of attorney terminates automatically on the death of the principal, or when the principal's agent and any third parties involved receive news of the principal's death. A future power of attorney that went into effect when the principal became incapacitated terminates automatically if the physician who certified the incapacity certifies that the principal has regained competence. A power of attorney automatically terminates if the agent resigns or dies and no successor agent was named in the original document. Moreover, a power of attorney can be terminated by court order if a claim is made and proven—by a beneficiary, for example—that the principal was incompetent when the power of attorney was executed.

Although the power of attorney generally avoids probate-court intervention in order to deal with disability, it cannot prevent disaffected family members from later seeking appointment of a guardian or a conservator. (In selecting a guardian or conservator, the court may, however, give priority to the agent named in the power of attorney.) Despite this limitation, though, a power of attorney, especially the durable power of attorney, is a useful, effective, and inexpensive means of preparing for disability.

■ ISSUES OF LIFE AND DEATH

There are two documents that can express your preferences about medical treatment or its cessation, the living will and the medical power of attorney. The living will explicitly states your preferences about medical treatment should you become unable to express them when suffering from a terminal illness. The medical power of attorney names another person who will have the right to make medical decisions for you if you become incapable of making them yourself. Both of these documents are sometimes called advance directives.

□ The Living Will

Most of us hope our death will be swift or painless, but not everyone will be that lucky. Accidents or diseases like cancer and AIDS often lead to physical and/or mental deterioration. Increasingly sophisticated life-support systems intended to maintain a patient's vital processes during difficult surgery or while diseases run their course can be used to prolong by days or months or even indefinitely the lives of patients whose condition is obviously hopeless—sometimes extending the agony of the patient, and nearly always resulting in high medical bills. Many individuals, if faced with such a situation, would prefer a quick and relatively painless death to additional suffering and expense.

The Right to Die □

The law distinguishes between active and passive euthanasia. Active euthanasia involves the deliberate administration of lethal doses of medication or any other intentional act undertaken to end a terminal patient's life, and is illegal everywhere.[1] Humanitarian motives are not a defense, so if you implore a doctor or friend to end your suffering by killing you, you are soliciting the commission of an illegal act, though your request will not necessarily go unheeded.

Passive euthanasia involves the refusal of treatment. It is well-established that all patients have the right to be fully informed of the risks and outcomes of every medical procedure, and to refuse treatment. This is known as "informed consent." Thus, if a doctor tells you that you have cancer and suggests that radiation or surgery can prolong your life, you may, provided you are mentally competent, reject the suggested treatment. The right of a patient to refuse medical treatment, even when such refusal means certain death, is absolute.

The right to refuse treatment, however, is useless if the patient is comatose or otherwise incompetent. In some states such cases are covered by "right to die" laws, which specify the circumstances under which treatment may be withheld, and designate individuals empowered to make the decision to withhold treatment. In states without right-to-die laws, though, the procedure for withholding treatment can be so complex that the patient often dies before a decision can be reached.

Right-to-die laws, though they differ from state to state, are designed to protect both the patient and the doctor. They protect the patient's right to a dignified death by permitting the refusal of further medical treatment—essentially a reiteration of the principle of informed consent. And they protect the doctor who authorizes passive euthanasia from criminal or civil liability that might otherwise result from his or her decision. All states with right-to-die laws require consensus by a group of physicians as well as the patient's family before treatment may be withheld.

Regardless of the laws of your state, if you would prefer to have your life terminated by passive euthanasia, the most effective instrument available to you is a living will, a document that expresses your preference clearly and formally. In states that have right-to-die laws, a properly executed living will is legally binding on your survivors and doctor. Moreover, in these states, the execution of a living will cannot be interpreted as suicide—important because insurance policies often contain a clause rendering the policy void if the insured commits suicide.

In states without right-to-die laws, living wills may not be legally binding. Nevertheless, a living will clearly expresses your preferences to your partner, your family, and your doctor. This can be extremely important because in some cases both the soon-to-be survivors and the doctor would prefer to discontinue life support, but feel restrained by their uncertainty as to the preference of the now-incompetent patient.

Drafting a Living Will □

Although wording for a living will varies from state to state, the following instructions should produce a legally acceptable document. The wording should generally follow the sample shown in the appendix.

Your living will should be dated, and the signing should be witnessed by two persons who are not beneficiaries or related to any beneficiaries of the signer and are not the signer's physician or employees of that physician.

Some states do not regard a living will as legally binding unless executed after the patient has been diagnosed as terminal. Thus, it is wise to change the date on your living will annually and then initial the change.

Many hospitals urge patients to execute a living will on admission for almost any but the most routine surgical procedures. In any event, copies should be given to your doctor for filing with your medical record, to one or more members of your family, to your domestic partner, and perhaps to a trusted (and younger) friend. The original, along with a list of all persons who have received copies, should be kept with your will, your letter of instruction, and other important papers.

The Medical Power of Attorney □

According to the laws of many states, in the absence of a living will the termination of life-support measures requires written consent, which obviously cannot be obtained from an individual who is comatose or otherwise incapable of communicating his or her wishes. Some states delegate decision making in such instances to the patient's parents or next of kin— a classification that does not include domestic partners, no matter how close or long-lived the relationship. Consequently, many gays and lesbians choose to execute a medical power of attorney (see sample form in the appendix).

A medical power of attorney authorizes a person of your choice to make all medical decisions for you in the event you become incapable of communicating such decisions yourself. The document, which goes into effect as soon as it is signed and witnessed, retains for you the right to make medical decisions as long as you are competent, and transfers this right to the person of your choice if and when you become incapacitated.

The living will, although a useful document, deals only with the question of life or death, and not other medical issues. The medical power of attorney, on the other hand, can deal with a wide range of medical issues. Moreover, it puts the decision making in the hands of someone who knows you intimately and is aware of your preferences. Although you should not designate more than one person, it's wise to select an alternate should your original designee be unable or unwilling to serve when the need arises.

The person you designate—sometimes called a patient advocate or surrogate—can be any adult. The individual should clearly understand your wishes and be willing to defend them in the face of what may be strong opposition from family or physician. There is no prohibition against designating the same person named in your financial power of attorney. Most states prohibit the appointment of your physician. Some states extend that prohibition to anyone caring for you in a hospital or to any beneficiary of your will. Thus, although your domestic partner may be your preferred choice as patient advocate, in some states you are not permitted to make such a designation if he or she is a beneficiary of your will.

Because the medical power of attorney can be far more detailed than a living will, you should give your agent as clear an understanding as possible regarding what treatments you prefer to accept or reject in specific circumstances. If you have a massive stroke, for example, do you want to reject aggressive treatment (such as mechanical ventilation or tube feeding) immediately? Or would you prefer your patient advocate allow such treatment initially, to be terminated later if ineffective? Or do you want to receive treatment for as long as possible? Because it allows you to make all sorts of specifications, the medical power of attorney is far more useful than the living will.

If you are away from home in another state, your medical power of attorney and your living will may or may not be honored, depending on the laws of that state. They are almost never honored by emergency medical technicians, who by law must presume your consent, stabilize you, and get you to a hospital. Once you are there, however, your medical power of attorney can be relied on in the event you are unable to make or communicate health-care decisions.

Although the legal requirements for a medical power of attorney differ from one state to another, you do not necessarily need the help of a lawyer in executing it. Forms are usually available from your hospital, your local bar association, or the state office on aging. Generic forms, which may not conform with your state's laws, should be avoided. (Forms that conform with the laws of your state are available free of charge from Choice in Dying, located at 200 Varick St., New York, NY 10014 (1-800-989-9455).

Once you have executed a medical power of attorney, you should make several copies and distribute them to your physician and anyone else with an interest in your welfare. Store the original in a safe place, making sure to tell your loved ones where it is stored.

Unfortunately, there is no ironclad guarantee that either your living will or your medical power of attorney will be honored. In some states, health-care providers are entitled to refuse to comply with it on moral or religious grounds. Some states require an objecting physician to remove himself or herself from the case and transfer it to someone willing to honor the documents, but this is not easily done. In some cases the hospital's ethics committee may resolve the problem; in others, a lawsuit may be necessary. This is why your patient advocate should be someone who does not shrink from conflict.

■ FUNDING LONG-TERM NURSING CARE

Although the problem of paying for health care in the event of a prolonged illness is one that everyone may face, gay or lesbian domestic partners might have additional concerns if they lack the approval and support of their family.

Because eligibility for Medicaid-funded nursing care is uncertain, and because neither Medicare nor the various Medigap policies cover all costs associated with a prolonged stay in a hospital, nursing home, or hospice, payment from other sources is almost essential.

Medicaid □

Medicare and Medigap do not pay for nursing-home care beyond 100 days. Medicaid, a federal program administered by the states, is available for the payment of services not covered by Medicare or Medigap. But eligibility for Medicaid requires a low net worth; the threshold is set by the state in which you reside. In general, you may own your house, its contents up to a limit of $2,000, your car valued at not more than $5,000, a $2,000 burial plot, and life insurance worth up to $1,500.

Medicaid's low net worth threshold has caused many people to rearrange their financial affairs to qualify. Assets are given away, converted from nonexempt to exempt assets, or transferred to a Medicaid qualifying trust.

A Medicaid qualifying trust transfers control of an individual's assets to a trustee, and gives the trustee authority to make support payments on behalf of the person establishing the trust. On the person's death the assets are distributed to beneficiaries named in the trust. Increasing numbers of upper- and middle-income people have taken advantage of this type of trust, but both Congress and the states have recently taken steps to limit its use. There is a possibility that in the future it may be completely prohibited.

☐ Long-Term Health-care Insurance

When first sold a number of years ago, long-term health-care insurance policies were generally unsatisfactory because insurers were uncertain about the extent of their payoffs and their exposure to liability. Recently, as a result of competition and government monitoring, benefits have improved significantly. But there is still no uniform format for these policies. Thus, any long-term care policy should, before purchase, be closely examined with respect to the following issues.

☐ The Benefits "Trigger"

The "trigger" is the event or condition that must occur to start the benefits. There are two approaches to triggering, functional and medical. The functional model identifies six activities of daily living and allows benefits to be paid when the insured can no longer perform a specified number—usually three of the six—without assistance. The medical model requires care to be "medically necessary" before benefits become payable.

☐ Levels of Care

Long-term health-care insurance policies generally offer three levels of care: custodial assistance; skilled care (daily care by professionals under a physician's supervision); and an intermediate level somewhere in-between. Lower levels of care may be provided at the patient's home or in an institutional setting. Higher levels are almost always provided in a nursing home.

Any policy you choose should provide care at all levels, both at home and in a nursing facility. It should not require that you use a lower level of care before becoming eligible for a higher one. A good policy will offer access to any level of care at any time.

Daily Benefit Amount ☐

The premium of a policy is based on the daily payment to which the insured is entitled when policy benefits are triggered. Before choosing the benefit amount, you should inquire about the cost of nursing-home care and what contribution, if any, can be expected from Medicaid.

Duration of Benefits ☐

Every policy sets a time limit on payment of benefits, usually one, two, or five years, and sometimes a lifetime. The longer the benefit period, the higher the premium. Before making a choice, assess your situation. Bear in mind that the average length of nursing-home care is between two and three years, and only a small percentage of patients remain in care more than five years.

Other Issues ☐

Other conditions of a policy that need careful scrutiny are the waiting period—the length of time before benefits begin—and the existence of a condition prior to the purchase of the policy. A pre-existing condition should not postpone benefits for more than six months. An "excluded impairments" clause, on the other hand, denies benefit payments for any conditions that existed at the time the policy was issued. Unless the policy contains a "waiver of premium" clause, you will have to continue paying the premium after benefits begin.

■ SUMMING IT UP

If domestic partners wish to empower one another to deal with possible future disability or incapacity, a financial power of attorney and a medical power of attorney are generally the tools of choice. If assets are substantial and likely to need management, the revocable living trust allows for professional management during life and is an excellent probate-avoidance device at death. If extended care seems likely, domestic partners should consider purchasing long-term health-care insurance.

Notes

[1]   Oregon law permits physician-assisted suicide in strictly limited circumstances.

Chapter 7

WHEN DEATH IS IMMINENT

I f you die suddenly, whatever estate plans you have made or funeral preferences you have expressed are irrevocable. But most of us don't die suddenly or unexpectedly; either we die of "natural causes" at an advanced age, or we die of a terminal illness.

Learning that you have only a few more months of life is, of course, a devastating experience, but psychologists and others who have studied people in such situations report that after a period of severe emotional upset a state of tranquil resignation almost inevitably evolves. Upon reaching that stage, the dying person uses his or her remaining time to "put things in order" with respect to family and other relationships, to fine-tune his or her estate plan, and to make last-minute transfers and beneficiary changes that reduce probatable assets and death taxes. The dying individual may also relieve family and friends of responsibility by making decisions about future medical treatment (or its withdrawal), and more precise funeral plans than it was practical to make when the time and location of death were remote and uncertain.

If you are stricken with a terminal illness, the likelihood that you will be able to take advantage of these last-minute opportunities will depend in large part on your relationship with your domestic partner, your family, your doctor, and your lawyer. Doctors are notoriously reluctant to tell a patient that death is approaching because they see such a statement as an admission of personal defeat, because such predictions often turn out to be wildly inaccurate, and because they believe such a statement will demoralize the patient.

Some doctors inform the domestic partner or family of a patient's imminent death, but families and lovers may be just as reticent as doctors to pass this information to the patient, especially if they share the doctor's concern about the patient's morale. And, even if both they and the patient know the patient's life is about to end, they may feel discussion about withdrawal of medical treatment, funeral details, or estate planning and property distribution is in poor taste.

This reticence on the part of doctor and family is not easy to overcome. But if you have executed a living will and a medical power of attorney, and if you have informed your doctor that you want to be told the truth at all times, and if you have usually responded rationally to bad medical news, then you are considerably more likely to be forewarned of your imminent death.

Once you know death is imminent, the advantage you can take from such knowledge is considerable, but your own reactions can create problems. The awareness that you are going to die can turn your thoughts so thoroughly inward that you may have none for the welfare of your survivors. Or you may become too depressed or angry to be able to function rationally. But most people do become reconciled, and many of them derive considerable comfort from the opportunity for last-minute decisions that will either benefit their survivors directly or, at the very least, reduce the number or the difficulty of the tasks that will face them immediately after the death.

Not everything suggested in the following pages will be appropriate or even feasible for you. Setting up a trust or writing a will, for example, involves at least two sessions with your lawyer, which may have to take place at your bedside. Still, with cooperation from your domestic partner, your family, your doctor, your lawyer, and perhaps your accountant, you will probably be able to accomplish more than you may expect.

MATTERS OF LIFE AND DEATH ■

Your Will □

If the value or the kind of property you own has changed significantly since you last made your will, or if the membership of your survivor group has changed, now is the time to review and update your will. You will want to make sure your will disposes of your property completely and according to your wishes. (Before making or revising your final will, you should consider the advantages of making some "lifetime gifts," discussed later in this chapter.) Other last-minute revisions might include a change in the nomination of your personal representative, the guardian of your minor children, a conservator, or the trustee of any trusts you have established.

If the revisions you plan to make are simple and few, there is no need to have your will redrawn. A codicil (see Appendix) will serve just as well.

Changing the beneficiaries in order to take account of changes in the membership of your survivor group is obviously sensible. But changing beneficiaries on an emotional basis is unwise. Although individuals who know they are terminally ill often review their lives and achieve a more balanced perspective of their relationships with partners, friends, and relatives—a perspective that may lead to the forgiving of old injuries, real or imagined, and to a more rational view of old feuds and grudges—other individuals can become embittered about their fate and review life in terms of slights, feuds, and failed relationships. Such a person may express his or her unhappiness vindictively in his or her will, perhaps disinheriting an otherwise favored relative for failure to visit as frequently as the dying person would like. In any event, if you make arbitrary changes in your beneficiaries, you run the risk of having your will contested. In such a situation, you would do well to protect the will against contest by following the procedures described in Chapter 1.

Perhaps the best advice one can give a terminally ill person is to make any beneficiary changes from charitable rather than vindictive motives. This advice might not prevent an impulsive and excessively generous gift to a nurse or housekeeper for personal services that a more objective observer would consider entirely routine, but it will prevent disinheritances or slights that the dying person would otherwise regret.

Holographic and Oral Wills ☐

Redrawing your will or writing a codicil usually involves the services of a lawyer and the presence of signing witnesses. If circumstances make this difficult or impossible, you might consider preparing a holographic will, currently recognized in 26 states. This informal will must be written entirely in your own handwriting and must contain no erasures or corrections. You must sign and date it, but your signing need not be witnessed.

If you live in a state that does not recognize holographic wills (see page 13), don't prepare one assuming that it might be "better than nothing." It will not be valid. You will be regarded as having died intestate unless you left a prior valid will. A holographic will can, even if invalid, communicate your wishes to your survivors, although it is not binding in any way. Even if you live in a state that recognizes holographic wills, we recommend a formal will. A formal will is likely to be more thoroughly reflective of your wishes and less likely to be contested. Oral wills, video wills, and deathbed statements have no legal standing in any state.

☐ Your Living Will

This is also the time to write, revise, or revoke your living will and/or your medical power of attorney. Imminent death may well change your earlier decisions about prolonging your life. The pain you suffer may be greater than anticipated, or the cost of your continued hospitalization may cause your survivors more hardship than a few weeks or months of extended, and, possibly quite painful life are worth to you. On the other hand, you may find that each day is precious, and that you want to remain alive for as long as possible.

If imminent death persuades you to make a living will or medical power of attorney, all you need do is copy the sample form shown in the appendix (if it complies with your state's laws), and sign it in the presence of two witnesses. Even if your state does not recognize these documents, they will communicate your wishes to your physician and loved ones. If you wish to revoke either document, simply destroy the original and notify your physician and loved ones that you have done so.

☐ Your Life Insurance

If you have life insurance, you may want to consider cashing in your policy or policies to pay medical bills or provide immediate funds that are otherwise needed. Under what is known as a viatical settlement, insurance companies, viatical companies, and brokers (who sell the policies to investors) will buy your policy for a substantial fraction of its face value once a doctor certifies your illness is terminal. The advantages of such an arrangement are that you, rather than your survivors, collect the proceeds and that you pay no income tax on the money you receive, provided you deal with a licensed company.

This cashing in of your policy is essentially a bet. The purchasing company is betting you will die quickly (thus ensuring a profit for the company, which, on your death, gets the face value of your policy) and you are betting you will live long enough to use the money for whatever purpose you need or want. Although viatical settlements were primarily developed for persons with AIDS, they are also available to patients suffering from other potentially terminal illnesses such as cancer, Alzheimer's, and Lou Gehrig's disease. They may also be available to elderly people, even those in good health.

The percentage of the face value you can collect on your policy varies widely but can be as high as 85 percent. Initially, when death from AIDS was likely to occur a very short time after diagnosis, the collectible percentage tended to be high. The percentage has dropped, however, as new and more effective drugs have been introduced, prolonging the lives of PWA's (persons with AIDS). Currently the rates vary sufficiently to justify shopping around. This can be done easily by calling either the National Viatical Association (1-800-741-9465) or the Viatical Association of America (1-800-842-9811).

At the time of this writing, the average life expectancy of people utilizing viatical settlements is about 20 months, and those individuals receive about 70 percent of their policies' death benefit. Someone diagnosed as having 12 months to live might collect as much as 85 percent, whereas someone with a life expectancy of five years might collect only 50 percent.

As tempting as the prospect of immediate cash may be, you need to be very careful before committing to a viatical settlement. You should have a clear idea of whether you really need the money now and what you will do with it.

Viatical companies are obligated to inform you of your options, including one called accelerated death benefits—an arrangement made with the life insurance company. Because viatical companies operate on a "buyer beware" principle, it is essential that you consult with your state insurance commissioner to make certain that any company you deal with is licensed in your state—otherwise you will be taxed on the benefits you receive. Before signing any viatical contract, you should get advice from your lawyer and/or your accountant.

For some patients, viatical payments are a godsend—funding, for example, the purchase of expensive drugs. For others they may be nothing more than a way to diminish the size of their estate at a considerable discount.

■ FUNERAL PLANNING

When death is imminent and the prospect of a funeral becomes a reality, people react in widely different ways. Some find the notion of making specific funeral plans grotesque. Others derive comfort from the opportunity to plan in detail their funeral service and the disposal of their remains.

The nearer you are to death, the more feasible detailed planning. You are less likely to move to another community or die far from home. It also becomes possible to negotiate funeral and burial (or cremation) arrangements in terms of their real dollar costs, since inflation is unlikely to change the cost appreciably. You also know which of your loved ones are likely to survive you and consequently be there to take responsibility for final arrangements, as well as how much money will be available to pay for those arrangements. You can speak with your clergyman or eulogist, a representative of the funeral home or memorial society, or anyone else involved in your plans to make certain every detail is as you wish. This kind of pre-arrangement is discussed further in Chapter 8.

If you do not wish to engage in such planning, there is no reason why you shouldn't leave it in the hands of whichever survivors will be ultimately responsible. This does not, however, mean the subject should not be discussed. If you ignore planning entirely, your survivors are likely to overspend on your funeral. Funeral directors are often able to exploit their customers, who are not only grief-stricken (and hence unable to make rational decisions) but also under enormous time pressure (and hence unable to do any comparison shopping). If your approaching death is openly acknowledged, however, you can urge your survivors to begin making arrangements in a more leisurely and rational way.

If you have expressed your preferences in your letter of instruction, there is no need to do anything more than give it— or at least the part dealing with funeral arrangements—to your survivors, perhaps with a suggestion that the time has come for making definite plans. If you have changed your mind about the funeral ritual or the method of body disposal since writing the letter, you should amend the letter to reflect your current thinking.

You also may have changed your mind about anatomical gifts. Your own illness may have heightened your sympathy for people with conditions your anatomical gifts might alleviate, or for the need of scientists for anatomical materials in their research on certain conditions.

■ MATTERS OF MONEY

With respect to your estate, there are five steps you should consider taking as death draws near.

1) Revise your letter of instruction, or make an inventory of your current assets and liabilities, as both may have changed significantly over time, especially during your final months.

2) Review the various probate-avoidance and tax-avoidance tactics described in Chapters 4 and 9. Consider transferring solely owned assets into such arrangements as joint ownership, pay-on-death accounts, and revocable living trusts, or shifting assets from one form of ownership to another to maximize the advantages each provides.

3) Consider the possibility of disposing of your estate by giving away as much of it as possible before your death—an effective way of avoiding both probate administration and federal estate tax.

4) Take care of administrative details that can be handled more easily while you're alive than by your survivors at a later date.

5) Review your will to determine whether its provisions have become moot or otherwise affected by anything you may have done in steps 1 through 4.

The following pages describe these five steps in detail. Not every suggestion will be relevant to your situation, but a careful reading is almost certain to uncover some simple measures that can save your survivors time, trouble, taxes, lawyer's fees, and court costs.

Inventorying Your Current Assets and Liabilities □

If you have not yet prepared a letter of instruction, now is the time to do so. If you already have one, it needs to be updated with a listing of your current assets, debts, and insurance benefits. If your illness has been lengthy, a portion of your assets may have been used to pay medical expenses or to meet household expenses if your illness interrupted your earnings.

Perhaps your stockbroker, if he or she has discretionary power, may have bought or sold securities since you became ill. You may also have some assets—a secret bank account, for example—that you have hitherto concealed from your domestic partner or family. (This list of assets is likely to change again before your death, requiring yet another revision of your letter, if you follow the property-transfer procedures outlined later in this chapter.)

Because your life insurance proceeds may represent a major portion of your total estate, you should make certain your survivors know where each policy is located and whether it is still in force. Otherwise your survivors might discard an old policy that looks as though it has lapsed, not realizing that premiums paid earlier may have kept it in force, though possibly at a reduced face value, or that the premiums were paid in full many years earlier.

It is also important to make sure your designation of life-insurance beneficiaries, both primary and contingent, is up to date. If you would like to place conditions or limitations on use of the proceeds, you may be able to set up a life-insurance trust, naming it the recipient of some or all of your life insurance proceeds. You may then designate who will receive assets from the trust, under what conditions, and when. Do not name your estate as a beneficiary on your policies, because doing so makes the insurance proceeds subject to probate and, if applicable, to state inheritance tax, whereas naming the trustee of an insurance trust as beneficiary does not.

If you live in a state that permits the sale of life insurance policies without medical examination, or if you belong to a credit union that schedules open-enrollment periods for group life insurance, also without medical examination, you may be able to buy more coverage, even in your present condition. If this is possible, don't let your conscience trouble you on grounds that you are committing fraud; you can be sure the premiums are calculated to take your situation into account.

☐ Last-Minute Probate and Tax Avoidance

Updating the inventory of your assets can help you determine whether they will require probate administration and whether your estate will be subject to federal estate tax. If you classify all your assets as either probate or non-probate, you can probably transfer the probate assets into alternative forms of ownership that avoid probate, such as a revocable living trust or a "pay-on-death" bank account. These devices, described in Chapter 4, exempt your assets from probate administration but do not remove them from your control while you are alive—an important consideration if there is any possibility you might recover.

Although your preparation of an inventory is likely to disclose probate assets, it is less likely to tell you if your estate is subject to federal estate tax. Because gay and lesbian domestic partners cannot take advantage of the estate tax unlimited marital deduction available to legally married spouses, and because the estate tax is imposed on nonprobate as well as probate assets, you need to consult the table on page 177 to determine whether the value of your taxable estate plus taxable gifts made during your lifetime exceeds the current exemption of $650,000.

Because the face value of your life insurance policies will be included as part of your estate-tax liability, you might consider transferring the ownership of these policies to your domestic partner or a friend. The person to whom you transfer the policies becomes responsible for paying the premiums, but your designation of the beneficiaries remains unchanged and your tax liability is avoided.

□ Giving Away Your Assets

If your taxable estate is large enough to be subject to the federal estate tax—or if you simply want to reduce your probate assets—you might consider reducing its value by making outright gifts or by transferring assets into a custodial account for minors, a trust for minors, or some other form of irrevocable transfer. Each of these gifts, to be free of federal gift tax, cannot exceed $10,000 in value annually. But there is no limit to the number of such gifts you can make. The disadvantage of such gifts is that they are irrevocable. If you transfer substantial assets and subsequently recover from what was thought to be a terminal condition, you could find yourself penniless or dependent on your beneficiaries.

Giving away your assets need not involve anything more than the paperwork necessary to set up a bank account. In addition, the recipients can express their gratitude while you are still able to enjoy it, and you may well derive pleasure from witnessing the uses to which they put your gifts.

You are entitled to make as many tax-free gifts of $10,000 as you like, provided you make no more than one per year to any recipient. But since the IRS uses a calendar year in its application of the annual exclusion, there is no reason why you can't make a tax-free gift to a recipient on December 31 and then follow it with another to the same recipient on January 1.

To be eligible for the annual $10,000 gift tax exclusion, the gift must be of a "present interest." In other words, it must be immediately usable (though not necessarily used) by the recipient. Gifts to a revocable living trust, since they are by definition revocable during your lifetime, are not gifts of a present interest and consequently remain subject to the estate tax.

For each annual gift exceeding $10,000, you must file a gift tax return and pay any tax due. In computing the gift tax, however, you first deduct the $10,000 annual exclusion from the value of the gift. If the reduced taxable value of your gift does not exceed your "unified gift and estate tax credit," you pay no tax. Upon your death, any unused portion of the unified credit can be used to reduce federal estate tax.

There is no limit on the number, size, or frequency of tax-free gifts you may make to charitable organizations provided the recipient organization is tax-exempt.

These rules make it possible for you to give away virtually everything you possess, not only to a domestic partner and next of kin, but to friends, charitable organizations, and anyone else you choose. In fact, by gifting off your assets you can carry out the provisions of your will while you are still alive and at the same time avoid probate. These lifetime gifts, however, are irrevocable, a reality you must consider carefully before transferring substantial assets beyond your control.

When you make such gifts, assets whose ownership is evidenced by written documents—securities, bank accounts, real estate, for example—will require documentary evidence reflecting the new ownership—new signature cards in the case of bank accounts, new stock certificates or a change on the registration of brokerage accounts, and new property deeds to establish retitling of real estate. But even transfers of unregistered possessions—jewelry, a coin collection, antiques, a painting—should be documented to show transfer to the new owner. This can be accomplished by use of a printed bill of sale, a form available from office supply stores. Despite its name, the bill of sale need not indicate that money was exchanged; it merely contains a description of the item(s), and the name of the original owner (the grantor or assignor) and the new owner (the grantee or assignee).

If you cannot conveniently obtain a printed bill of sale form for use in gifting items of personal property, you may write or type your own assignment form, provided you identify the gifted asset(s), the assignee, and your intent to make the transfer, all followed by the date and your signature. An example of a typical assignment form for personal property is:

I give and assign my coin collection and my Jasper Johns painting to my son, Joseph Jones.
Date:
Signature:

□ Think Before You Give

The procedures described above can offer you satisfaction from both an economic and a psychological point of view. In economic terms, they enable you to maximize the effectiveness of your estate planning by minimizing the erosion of your estate by probate administration costs and death taxes. The psychological benefits may be even more substantial. When death seems imminent, a review of one's life is almost inevitable—and the quality of one's life is measurable not only in terms of personal relationships, but also, in our society, by material assets. For some individuals, the revision of their will and the making of lifetime gifts constitutes a very real reassurance that their life has been worthwhile.

On the other hand, as we noted earlier, the prospect of death can easily distort perspective and precipitate a number of actions that are ill advised. Thus, the prospect of giving away your assets while you are still alive and can experience the recipients' gratitude, not to mention the additional pleasure of outwitting tax authorities, may tempt you to reduce your estate to almost nothing. Bear in mind, though, that it may be better to retain control of your estate and reserve the opportunity to change your mind, even if this results in your beneficiaries' having to pay probate costs and death taxes.

In addition, the recommendations in this chapter are based on the assumption that when death is near, your domestic partnership is stable and your family structure is unlikely to change. This may not be the case. Before transferring ownership of the bulk of your assets to a domestic partner, a family member, or anyone else, you must be totally confident that the objects of your generosity will not use your gifts in ways in which you do not approve.

Lastly, as we pointed out at the beginning of this chapter, the doctor who predicted that you will die shortly may just possibly be wrong. Completed lifetime gifts are irrevocable, and, if your beneficiaries are not totally trustworthy, you could find yourself miraculously restored to good health but financially destitute as a consequence of your own generosity. For this reason you may be well advised to use a revocable living trust or pay-on-death bank account as a means of avoiding probate, as such techniques allow you to revoke or modify the arrangement at any time before you die.

☐ Making Things Easier for Your Survivors

A number of matters that will become the responsibility of your survivors after your death can be attended to more easily and more flexibly while you are alive.

The ownership of your motor vehicles, for example, is more easily transferred by you than by your survivors. Although most states provide survivors with a relatively simple process for transferring vehicle titles after death, these procedures almost invariably place a maximum limit on the value of the vehicle and often are available only to spouses or heirs at law and consequently not to gay or lesbian domestic partners. While you are alive, however, you can transfer a vehicle of any value to anyone you please simply by signing the certificate of title and delivering it to the assignee.

The transfer of jointly owned property to the surviving joint owner also involves certain formalities if it is done after your death. If you make these transfers while you are alive, you may save your survivors both time and trouble. If, for example, you own stock certificates in your own name or jointly, it may make sense to have your broker transfer them into the broker's "street account." Once this is done, you need merely change ownership on the broker's street account instead of on each stock certificate.

If you rent a safe deposit box, whether jointly or in your

name alone, banks in some states, on hearing of your death, are required to seal the box to prevent further access until a representative of the state treasury department arrives to inventory the contents for tax purposes. All unregistered contents may be presumed to belong to you, and will therefore be subject to probate and to estate taxes.

For this reason, it may be advisable to empty the box of all contents not registered solely in your name and perhaps to rent another box in the name of a joint owner into which the valuables may be stored until they are disposed of. If the box you have rented is in your name alone, a domestic partner, a family member, or a trusted friend can access it while you are alive if you provide him or her with a power of attorney or with an authorization form some banks provide for this purpose.

Although the avoidance of probate is generally advisable, there are a few situations in which passing assets through probate is desirable. If, for example, you own jointly with your domestic partner one hundred shares of a stock for which you paid $10 a share, but which are now worth $20, the shares will pass to him or her automatically on your death. But when he or she sells the shares, the capital gain will be calculated on the basis of their original cost of $10, regardless of their value at the time of your death. If, on the other hand, these shares were solely owned by you and he or she acquired them through inheritance, his or her cost basis would be the stock's "stepped up" value at the time of your death, $20. In short, for tax purposes the value of any inherited asset is calculated as its value at the time of the owner's death rather than its value at the time it was originally acquired. Thus, paying probate costs now might reduce capital gains taxes later.

☐ A Final Review of Your Will

If you have taken any of the actions suggested in the preceding pages, your will may no longer represent your intended distribution of your assets. If, for example, you have made a lifetime gift of your harpsichord to your daughter, there is no point in specifying it in the will as a bequest to her. A final review and revision of your will to delete bequests that are no longer relevant may serve not only to prevent future disputes among beneficiaries but to remind you of assets you may have overlooked or beneficiaries you may have neglected.

■ HOW IMPORTANT IS ALL THIS?

The suggestions and instructions in this chapter may well have given you the impression that the last days of your life should be spent with a calculator, tax tables, worksheets, all in the company of your lawyer or accountant in a desperate effort to attain absolute perfection in your estate planning, to avoid probate completely, and to minimize potential taxes. This, however, is not our intent.

To begin with, if you followed the suggestions offered in Chapters 1 and 4, your last-minute adjustments should involve only trivial odds and ends which, even if neglected, should not make a major difference to your survivors. Furthermore, in our society it is the responsibility of survivors to take care of both the physical and financial remains of their loved ones. Just as you or your siblings may have had to cope with the problems created by the deaths of your parents or other elderly relatives, so, too, those who love you can be expected to cope with yours. There is no need to be obsessively concerned with accounting for every last penny or every petty detail, or to be conscience-ridden by various bits of unfinished business.

The ending of life is a time for contemplation and for the repair or reinforcement of personal relationships. It would be unfortunate if you were to forgo these important activities for the sake of a possible reduction in taxes or the cost of probate administration.

Chapter 8

FUNERALS—AND SOME ALTERNATIVES

Planning the rituals and method of body disposal that mark your passing may strike you as morbid but, without at least some planning, the costs of a funeral and burial can substantially deplete the assets you leave behind. Hence, devoting some thought to what you would prefer when your life ends makes sense. Many individuals plan their funeral and burial down to the smallest detail, although that may not be the best approach. To begin with, unless you are terminally ill, the time, place, and circumstances of your death are uncertain. You may die thousands of miles from home; or the eulogist you have chosen may predecease you; or inflation may drive the cost of your plans far beyond the money you have set aside; or the membership of your survivor group may change through death, separation, or estrangement. Moreover, if you die in an accident—fire, drowning, plane crash—there may be no body for your survivors to dispose of.

There are other uncertainties as well. On your death, control of your body and the right to decide on its disposal pass to your next of kin and not to a friend or domestic partner. And your next of kin are under no obligation to comply with your or your domestic partner's wishes, even if money is available. Although a durable financial power of attorney empowers your agent to make preplanned arrangements during your incapacity, that power is revoked at death and cannot be used to dictate postmortem arrangements. It is even possible for a distraught or homophobic family to exclude a gay or lesbian partner from the ceremony and burial.

Given these obstacles, it is not really practical to make specific arrangements with a funeral home, cemetery, or monument firm. Because of continuous inflation, no reputable funeral home will write a future "preneed" contract specifying a price in current dollars. Even if you prepay a substantial amount for your funeral, your survivors may be faced with additional charges, or possibly a funeral much simpler than what you specified. It is also possible that the funeral home with which you contracted may have gone bankrupt or out of business, in which case your prepayment may be lost entirely.

Advance purchase of a cemetery plot, monument, or casket also presents problems. Many people believe the purchase of a cemetery plot represents a miniature investment in real estate, which can yield a profit if not ultimately used. But this is not the case. Ownership of a cemetery plot is not the same as ownership of your house and grounds. Ownership of a plot gives you the right to be buried there in a casket or a crematory urn, but, if you move or change your plans, you are, in some states, not permitted to sell it at a profit. And some cemeteries restrict resale rights to themselves. Monuments may also be purchased in advance, but what value will they have if you move before you die? They are expensive to ship, and their resale value is negligible. The same holds true for caskets.

You may feel the arguments presented above relieve you of any obligation to plan for your funeral but, although it may be inadvisable to formulate specific plans, it is important you make some general decisions and share them with your domestic partner, next of kin, and anyone else who might be involved with your final arrangements.

If your survivors are unaware of your preferences, they may be talked into the most expensive funeral they can afford. If you wanted an elaborate funeral, no harm will have been done. But if you would have preferred something simpler and less expensive, money that may have gone to your survivors may go instead to the funeral director.

A second reason for making and sharing your plans may be even more important. Your funeral is for the benefit of your survivors. It will be a significant event that at least some of them will remember for the rest of their lives. Thus, it is crucial not only that they be aware of your preferences but that you be aware of theirs—and perhaps modify yours to accommodate theirs if there are differences. We suggest you center your discussions on the following three general questions:

1) What kind of ritual do I want to mark my death?

Do you want your family and friends to "pay their last respects" by filing past your open casket and joining a cortege to the cemetery? Or do you want a memorial service without your body present? Or would you prefer a convivial party with music, drinks, and entertainment.

2) How concerned am I about keeping my body intact?

Your answer to this question will influence your decisions about cremation, donating your body or organs for research or transplanting, and various other options described later in this chapter. It may also influence your choice of casket and grave site if you believe—against all scientific evidence—that the right choice of casket can prevent decay.

3) How much will the disposal of my remains cost my survivors?

Even if, allowing for inflation, you set aside enough money for a traditional funeral, cemetery burial, and perpetual care, some of the money could, if you make a less expensive choice, pass to your survivors. From this point of view, then, you are not really "paying your own way." At the time of this writing the average funeral, including cemetery burial, costs approximately

$6,000. If this sum represents only a small fraction of your net worth, both you and your survivors may feel it is money well spent. But if your funeral expenses might be financially crippling to your survivors, a less costly alternative may be desirable.

Once you and those close to you have reached agreement, or at least an acceptable compromise, on answers to these fundamental questions, you can begin to examine specific alternatives. Some of your choices are related to actual disposal of your body, others to social rituals. Usually these two functions are independent of each other, but sometimes one of them places restrictions on the other. A church service with the body present, for example, can be easily followed either by grave burial or cremation but not by donation of the body for research. Organ donation for transplant can be followed by a viewing of the open casket, but body donation can be followed only by a memorial service. Since your body must ultimately be disposed of by one of only a few methods, whereas ritual is available in a wide variety of alternatives or can be dispensed with altogether, we shall review the disposal alternatives first, indicating any limitations they place on memorial rituals.

■ DISPOSAL ALTERNATIVES

□ Grave burial

Grave burials are so traditional in the United States that many people do not even consider the alternatives, and today the overwhelming majority of Americans make this choice. The arguments in its favor are so widely accepted they need only the briefest of mention.

A grave is believed to provide a "permanent" resting place. A family grave plot, or even adjoining graves, promise eternal togetherness for family members or domestic partners. And a grave, especially if it is situated in serene and attractive surroundings, is an inviting place for memorial visits by survivors.

A grave is not, however, permanent. Cemeteries can be and have been destroyed to make way for reservoirs, hydroelectric projects, superhighways, and other public works. Moreover, the togetherness provided by a family plot becomes less achievable in a society in which one out of five families changes its address every year and in which separation, estrangement, and other changes inevitably reduce people's concern for their ancestors. And even if families remain in place and loyal to the memory of their forebears, many grave sites that were initially serene and inviting become unattractive through overcrowding, urbanization, or neglect.

Those who oppose grave burial offer additional arguments. Cemeteries use land that might otherwise be put to more socially productive purposes. Cemetery plots are expensive, as are headstones. Cemetery burial is usually preceded by embalming, the purchase of an expensive casket, and other elaborate and costly services. Many people feel, also, that burial concentrates attention on the deceased's physical remains rather than on the meaning of his or her life.

☐ Cremation

Cremation, although chosen by only a small minority of Americans, is the most widely used disposal method in many countries—especially those, such as Japan and England, in which population density has made the use of land for cemeteries prohibitively expensive.

Some people are horrified by the very word "cremation." But a visit to a modern crematorium may allay their fears. Often resembling a conventional funeral home, with rooms available for viewing the body and for conducting funeral or memorial services, the crematorium contains a high-temperature furnace which, in a matter of two to three hours, reduces the body to approximately eight pounds of ash. Temperatures are so high that there is no smoke, and the ashes produced by the container or casket are completely consumed. The remaining bones are pulverized and combined with the body's ashes, and the "cremains" are placed in an urn or container.

There are several alternatives for disposal of your ashes. They may be buried in a conventional grave; most cemeteries permit the interment of two cremated bodies in a single grave, and charge less for the opening and closing of the grave than for a casket. Alternatively, the crematory urn may be kept permanently in a niche in a columbarium, usually operated by the crematorium. Some crematoria scatter the ashes in a memorial garden.

In some states, commercial operators—often the owners of private aircraft or seagoing vessels—are permitted to charge fees for scattering the ashes over land or waters specified in your letter of instruction or by your survivors. Other states prohibit the scattering of ashes, but it is difficult to see how such laws can be enforced if survivors scatter remains privately and inconspicuously.

None of these alternatives need be chosen before or immediately after cremation. Usually the survivors are given the cremains in a canister or urn, and ultimate disposition can occur at any time after that.

Cremation is supported by either or both of two arguments—one philosophical, the other economic. The philosophical argument is that cremation is swift, clean, and final, and that survivors are not stressed by thoughts about a body "moldering in the ground." Obviously, this argument is entirely subjective.

The economic argument is that cremation is far cheaper than grave burial because embalming is not necessary, a simple, inexpensive container can be used instead of a coffin, no cemetery plot or grave marker is needed, and, if death occurs away from home, it is less expensive to ship the cremains than a body.

But these economies are not inevitable since they deal only with the cremation process and not rituals. If, for example, cremation is chosen in conjunction with a traditional funeral, the full services of a funeral director may be required, and the only economy will be the difference between crematorium and cemetery costs. On the other hand, grave burial, if you choose a simple graveside service, need not involve the full range of services offered by funeral directors as part of the "standard adult funeral."

To compare the costs of cremation with those of grave burial you need to compare the cost of cremation, an urn, and (perhaps) placement of the urn in a columbarium or a grave against the cost of a cemetery plot, opening and closing costs, perpetual care or annual maintenance fees, and a casket.

If you have philosophical objections to cremation (only Orthodox Judaism actually prohibits it), the economic argument will probably leave you unmoved. If you have no preference, though, you may want to say so in your letter of instruction. Giving your survivors an option allows them to consider circumstances and costs at the time of your death.

☐ Direct Disposal

If you are not concerned with how your body is disposed of, or with a ritual that involves the presence of your body, you may be interested in direct disposal. Under this system, a commercial firm collects your body and transports it directly to a crematorium or cemetery. Because many of the services of a funeral director are eliminated or provided at a lower cost, these firms can provide complete service for about one-fourth the cost of a standard adult funeral. Memorial services or any other rituals remain the responsibility of your survivors.

☐ Body Donation

The donation of your body to a hospital or medical school for research or teaching purposes and the donation of your organs for transplant surgery are often considered as essentially the same process, but they are not. Although both procedures are covered by the Uniform Anatomical Gift Act (a law adopted by all states), they are for the most part mutually exclusive. If you decide to give any of your organs except your corneas for transplant purposes, your body becomes unacceptable for use in research or teaching. And if you give your body for research or teaching purposes, your organs cannot be used for transplant.

People who intend to donate their bodies to an institution for research or teaching do so to eliminate funeral costs and/or to benefit humanity. If your body has been mutilated or emaciated, though, it may not be usable for research or teaching. And because no institution can be compelled to accept an anatomical gift, it is important you make alternative plans for disposal.

Giving your body to a specific institution is also somewhat uncertain. The need for bodies is not as great as it used to be, and it is not uniform in all parts of the country. As a consequence, reciprocity among medical schools has developed and, as a result, your body might not end up at the institution of your choice.

Some medical schools will pick up your body from the place of death at no cost to your survivors. Others require that your survivors deliver it. None, however, will pay transportation costs if you die in a distant place. And, although you have the legal right to donate your body, most medical schools require written consent of your survivors before they will accept your gift.

If you wish to donate your body, you should indicate this

preference in your letter of instruction and on a Uniform Donor Card[1] Be sure to select an alternate method of disposal, however, in case your wishes cannot be carried out.

Most medical schools require that your body not be embalmed, though some will accept a body that has been embalmed according to their instructions. This restriction usually precludes any kind of service with the body present, and the usual practice is for survivors to hold a memorial service shortly after the death. After the body has served its purpose in research or teaching, it can be returned to the survivors for burial or cremation. In most cases, however, it is disposed of by the institution, usually by cremation, and the ashes are returned to the survivors if they wish.

☐ Organ Donation

In contrast to body donation, organ donation is not motivated by the desire to eliminate disposal costs, as it is not a method for final disposal. Thus, it in no way precludes a traditional service or viewing of the body. And, although the need for bodies fluctuates, the need for transplantable organs always exceeds the supply.

Donating your organs will almost inevitably prolong or improve someone's life. Your corneas, transplanted, will restore the recipient's sight. Each of your kidneys can give an otherwise doomed recipient new life. Your skin can help the recovery of burn victims, and numerous other organs can also be used in treatment or research.

Organ transplant is beset by two problems: most organs must be removed promptly after death, and a recipient who is biologically compatible with the donor must be located and readied for transplant shortly after the donor's death. Finding a biological and chronological "match" is not always easy. Doing so depends not only on the circumstances of your death but on the efficiency of the transplant network in your community. Hospitals that are part of such a network can, when a donor's death is impending, alert a recipient in the community or plan to quickly ship the donation to where it can be used.

One consideration that deters some people from becoming donors is the fear that their death will be hastened by physicians eager to get their organs for transplant. This fear is groundless. The code of ethics established for transplanting organs prohibits any physician involved in the transplant surgery from attending the potential donor.

Conversely, other people fear they will be kept alive artificially until a recipient can be located and prepared. This does occur. Most states now accept the concept of "brain death" (a "flat electroencephalograph" taken several times and indicating irreversible inactivity in the brain) as the definition of death. After death thus defined, it is possible to maintain circulation and respiration by artificial means, and this is sometimes done to keep organs available for transplant. The individual thus maintained, however, is, in fact and by law, dead.

Thus, just as it is difficult to donate your entire body to a specific institution for a specific use, it is difficult to donate a specific organ. A better plan if you intend to be a donor is to execute a Uniform Donor Card, indicating on it whatever options you prefer. Two of the options—body donation or organ donation—are mutually exclusive, but checking both allows the ultimate decision to be made considering the circumstances of your death, ensuring that your gift will be used optimally.

■ RITUAL ALTERNATIVES

☐ Type and Location of Service

The alternatives for rituals marking your death are virtually limitless, and their various features can be combined in a variety of ways. A religious service, for example, can be held in a house of worship, a funeral home, a crematorium, the deceased's or a survivor's home, or at the grave site and can be held with an open casket, a closed casket, or with no body present.

Memorial services can be held anywhere and at any time after the death, since they usually take place with no body present. As with body disposal, it is difficult to make precise arrangements before death occurs, but you should reach a general agreement with your domestic partner or next of kin on some of the following preferences.

☐ Choice of Casket

The cost of the casket is the largest component of total funeral costs, ranging from under two hundred to several thousand dollars. Your choice of casket becomes especially important if you are concerned with sparing expenses for your survivors.

There are two basic concerns when selecting a casket: social display and preservation of the body. Social display is so personal a consideration that no "objective" advice is possible other than the sometimes-overlooked fact that simplicity is always in good taste.

On the question of whether an expensive casket preserves the body, however, the objective answer is clear. It does not. Enough exhumations have been conducted to support the firm conclusion that no casket prevents decay. Furthermore, sealed metal caskets, often sold on the grounds that they postpone decay, may actually hasten it.

Many people combine economy with simplicity by ordering the Orthodox Jewish casket—a plain wooden box. Any funeral director can easily obtain one if he or she does not have one in stock.

Open or Closed Casket □

Viewing of the body has been the subject of considerable debate. Those in favor argue that viewing convinces survivors of the reality and finality of death and that many friends as well as relatives want the opportunity of a "last look." Those opposed point out that it places undue emphasis on the physical remains, that it indirectly increases funeral costs because it usually requires embalming and cosmetic restoration, and that it may induce survivors to choose a more elaborate casket.

If you are considering an open casket, bear in mind that at your death emaciation or disfigurement of your body may make you look somewhat less than presentable. Some morticians, working through photographs, achieve admirable restorations; others produce grotesque and irreparable caricatures.

□ Flowers or Other Tributes

You may want to discuss with your survivors the question of whether mourners should send flowers—the traditional method for mourners to express sympathy. On the other hand, you may feel flowers are a waste of money. If so, you should include in your letter of instruction that your obituary notice should request no flowers, possibly suggesting that, in lieu of flowers, a contribution be sent to a specified charitable or philanthropic organization.

□ Post-Funeral Rituals

Although it is not an integral part of the funeral, a post-funeral gathering of mourners, usually with food and drink, has become traditional. Its primary purposes are to provide support for those who are most severely bereaved and to offer an opportunity for relatives and friends to come together in a social way. Because there is no pre-scribed format for these occasions, you may wish to lay out some specifications of your own, keeping in mind that either your estate or survivors will pay for whatever gathering you plan.

■ MEMORIAL SOCIETIES

Memorial societies are becoming increasingly widespread. They originated as consumer cooperatives designed to reduce the high cost of funerals. Although memorial societies have aroused the hostility of the funeral industry, opposition has not prevented their spread. Today hundreds of such societies exist in the United States and Canada.

Memorial societies are dedicated to public service and are operated almost entirely by volunteers, but each differs somewhat in the way it functions. Some have formal contracts with one or more funeral homes. In return for the volume of business generated by the society, the funeral home(s) offer special prices, sometimes as much as 50 percent below the cost of a typical funeral. Others have no formal contracts but deal cooperatively with one or more funeral homes, continuously monitoring their service and prices. Still others simply provide members with information and advice when the need arises.

A one-time individual or family membership entitles you to the society's services and, because there is reciprocity among societies in various parts of the country, you do not necessarily lose the benefits of membership if you move.

When these societies originated, membership tended to be above average in income, education, and occupational prestige. Because members preferred the simplest possible alternatives for both ritual and disposal, memorial societies initially stressed an austere style at minimal cost. As they attempted to extend their membership, they recognized that members of other cultures and economic groups often had different preferences. As a consequence, many memorial societies have broadened the range and style of services they offer. The common denominator remains protection of members against financial exploitation.

You may be able to find your local memorial society in the Yellow Pages under "Memorial Societies" or by consulting a local clergyman. A centralized source of information is the Continental Association of Funeral and Memorial Societies at 1828 L Street NW, Washington, DC, 20036.

■ PLANNING TENTATIVELY

We have attempted in this chapter to present a broad overview of current ritual and body disposal practices and alternatives. Our purpose is to help you make general decisions. If you are seriously concerned about the costs of the kind of funeral you prefer, you might consider setting up an investment or fund specifically earmarked for your funeral and burial expenses, perhaps something designed to keep pace with inflation. An insurance policy bought for this purpose will not keep pace with inflation, but could net your estate a "profit" if you die before your premiums equal your policy's face value.

In general, the actual negotiations for funeral arrangements are best left to your survivors. The decisions you make prior to death should be tentative. Nevertheless, general decisions made after thoughtful discussion with your domestic partner, your children, and other potential survivors will make the ultimate planning of your funeral arrangements easier, relieving your loved ones of at least some of the stress occasioned by your death.

Notes

[1] Donor cards are available from the Kidney Foundation and other sources. Some state motor-vehicle administrations offer all licensed drivers the option of indicating an organ-donor preference on their driver's license so their intention to donate will be noticed promptly. But this intention is difficult to revoke should you change your mind, whereas a donor card can simply be destroyed.

Chapter 9

PROBATE AND TAXES

The probating of your estate, and the calculation and payment of death taxes will be the responsibility of your personal representative, but there are two reasons why both subjects deserve your attention now. First, now is the time when you can rearrange your assets to simplify or avoid both probate and death taxes. Second, if you have been nominated as the personal representative of another person—your domestic partner, for example, or a parent—you may need to cope with these issues while you are still alive.

For this chapter we will assume your domestic partner, a parent, or some other individual has died and you have been named personal representative of his or her estate.

THE PROBATE PROCESS ■

In theory, the probate process is both logical and useful. It works as follows. Upon the death of the person who nominated you as the personal representative, you appear before the county probate court (in some states called the surrogate or chancery court) and petition to be formally appointed as the estate's personal representative, and to certify that the deceased's will is valid.

Once your appointment is confirmed, the court issues you, the personal representative, a document called letters of authority. This document authorizes you to identify, collect, and manage all assets in the deceased's name—real estate, bank accounts, securities, plus any wages and other debts owed to the deceased—and to consolidate those assets into what is called the deceased's probate estate.

Once the court has preliminarily approved the deceased's will, any interested person can appear before the court to contest it. Although will contests are relatively rare, the will of a deceased gay or lesbian domestic partner may be especially subject to contest if the deceased partner's parents, siblings, or adult children have been alienated or if they resent the surviving partner. This possibility is good reason for gay and lesbian domestic partners to plan their estates to avoid probate.

Once the deceased's probate assets have been identified, collected, and inventoried, you, as personal representative, are obligated to complete the following steps:

1) Publish a newspaper notice to the deceased's creditors, notifying them to submit their claims against the estate by a specified date.

2) Pay all valid claims, using estate funds.

3) Continue any insurance and necessary maintenance on such estate assets as buildings and vehicles until these are sold or transferred to the entitled beneficiaries.

4) Calculate and pay all state and federal income and death taxes owed by the deceased and by the estate.

5) Distribute the remaining probate assets to the entitled beneficiaries according to the terms of the will (or, if there was no will, according to the state's intestacy law), after which the estate can be closed and you can be discharged.

The probate process is designed to ensure that all parties—creditors, beneficiaries, heirs at law, and the tax authorities—are treated fairly and receive what is coming to them. As praiseworthy as the probate process is in theory, though, its practice is so riddled with problems that knowledgeable domestic partners nearly always make serious efforts to avoid it.

A major problem with probate administration is delay. It is not uncommon for the probating of an estate to take several months. More complicated or contested estates can take years to settle. Meanwhile, the beneficiaries, heirs, and creditors cannot receive their due, and any ongoing business the deceased owned solely may come to a halt.

The expense of probate administration is also a serious concern. Even if, as personal representative, you agree to serve without fee, you will probably need to hire some combination of a lawyer, an accountant, an appraiser, and a realtor to settle the estate, with their fees paid from estate funds.

Worse yet, if the deceased failed to nominate a personal representative, the court will probably appoint someone other than the surviving domestic partner. If the court appoints a person or bank with no compelling interest in settling the estate promptly, the closing—and its associated costs—may drag on almost indefinitely. It is not uncommon for a relatively modest estate to be severely depleted during probate administration.

Although any interested party—a relative, for example, an unrelated beneficiary named in the will, or a creditor—can initiate probate proceedings, it is important to recognize that not all estates must undergo formal probate administration. To begin with, if the deceased left no probate assets, probate administration is not necessary. Even if there are probate assets, they may be of modest value and thus eligible for "small-estate" transfer procedures discussed in the next few pages.

Although it is likely the deceased left at least a few probate assets, some probatable items can be transferred to the entitled survivors without undergoing formal probate administration. The deceased's motor vehicles, for example, may have been registered solely in the deceased's name. If so, they are part of the probate estate. If their value does not exceed a specified amount, though, usually somewhere between $5,000 and $25,000, ownership can be quickly transferred to survivors specified in the will (or by state law if there is no will) simply by filling out a title transfer application provided by the state department of motor vehicles. Your state department of motor vehicles or secretary of state's office can explain whether the procedure is available and, if so, what it involves. Usually all the survivor need do is to present the vehicle's title, a certified copy of the death certificate, and a copy of the will. Once the survivor has signed an affidavit of inheritance, ownership of the vehicle can be transferred to the entitled beneficiary.

Any wages, vacation pay, and fringe benefits due the deceased from an employer are, strictly speaking, probate assets. However, in some states the employer may pay this money directly to specified kin—a spouse, child, or other heir at law but not a domestic partner.

In order to protect its interests, the employer may require a death certificate and an affidavit identifying the survivor and specifying his or her right to the money. The personnel departments of major corporations are generally familiar with this procedure, but small employers may not be. If problems are encountered, the probate court or your state's department of labor should be able to help. If survivors feel the employer is withholding or delaying payment, they can file a complaint with the state department of labor, file suit in small-claims court, or retain a lawyer.

☐ Appointment of Guardians for Minor Children

If the deceased is survived by a minor child or children, a guardian must be appointed by the probate court, although this does not necessarily mean the deceased's estate will be subject to probate administration. If children have been adopted jointly or born to one domestic partner and adopted by the other, no guardian need be appointed unless both partners die. If a surviving nonparent partner has been nominated as guardian in the deceased partner's will, his or her appointment is likely to be approved by the court, despite possible objection by the deceased's family, unless the surviving partner is shown to be unfit. If there was no will, a surviving nonparent domestic partner may petition for appointment as guardian, but a competing petition by relatives would be given serious consideration by the court and might very well prevail.

Wrongful-death Claims □

If the deceased died as a result of someone's negligent or wrongful act—for example, in a vehicle accident, in surgery, or as the result of an assault—the personal representative should investigate the possibility of pursuing a claim against whoever is responsible for the death. State laws permit recovery of damages for loss of companionship by the victim's surviving spouse, parents, or children, but not by a gay or lesbian domestic partner. This is yet another example of how gay and lesbian domestic partners enjoy less legal protection than their legally married, straight counterparts.

TWO SIMPLER FORMS OF PROBATE ■

Responding to widespread public complaints about the delays, costs, and occasional abuses inherent in full probate administration, state legislatures have adopted one or both of two simpler, quicker, and less expensive procedures designed specifically for the transfer at death of relatively small estates: transfer by affidavit, and transfer by summary probate administration. Both procedures are generally available only to surviving spouses or other heirs at law, but occasionally they can be used by anyone (including domestic partners) named in the deceased's will. To find out if your state allows domestic partners to utilize either of these procedures, contact your local probate court.

☐ Transfer By Affidavit

For the transfer of small estates—personal property not exceeding a specified limit, typically set between $5,000 and $20,000—many states offer a transfer-by-affidavit procedure that eliminates the need for a personal representative, formal probate court administration, and notification of the deceased's creditors.

The transfer affidavit, usually available as a printed form from the probate court, typically must state that the claimant is legally entitled to inherit the deceased's assets, the value of the deceased's estate less liens does not exceed the state-specified maximum, at least 30 days have elapsed since the death, and no petition for appointment of a personal representative is pending or has been granted.

Under the Uniform Probate Code (adopted by 15 states as of this writing), the affidavit transfer procedure can be used to transfer any personal property—bank accounts, money-market accounts, promissory notes, securities, household furnishings and equipment, the contents of safe deposit boxes—provided their total value falls within the state-specified limit. Under this procedure, in all but a few states, the deceased's creditors need not be notified or paid. Most states that have not adopted the Uniform Probate Code provide similar procedures. Transfer by affidavit procedures usually do not require the assistance of a lawyer.

One disadvantage of this simplified asset transfer procedure is that in most states it cannot be used to transfer real estate.

State Requirements For Small Estate Transfer by Affidavit				
State	Dollar Limitation ($)	Waiting Period Following Death (days)	Procedure Excludes Real Estate	Creditors Must First Be Paid
Alabama	Not Available			
Alaska[1]	15,000	30	Yes	No
Arizona[1]	30,000	30	Yes	Yes
Arkansas	Not Available			
California	60,000	40	Yes	No
Colorado[1]	27,000	10	Yes	No
Connecticut[1]	20,000	30	Yes	Yes
Delaware[1]	20,000	30	Yes	Yes
DC	Not Available			
Florida	Not Available			
Georgia	Not Available			
Hawaii[1]	20,000	30	Yes	No
Idaho[1]	25,000	30	Yes	No
Illinois	25,000	0	Yes	Yes
Indiana[1]	15,000	45	Yes	No
Iowa	Not Available			
Kansas	Not Available			
Kentucky	Not Available			
Lousiana[3]	50,000	0	Yes	Yes
Maine[1]	10,000	30	Yes	No
Maryland	Formula[4]	0	Yes	Yes
Massachusetts	Formula[5]	60	Yes	No
Michigan[1]	5,000	0	Yes	No
Minnesota	20,000	30	Yes	No
Mississippi	20,000	30	Yes	No
Missouri	15,000	30	No	Yes
Montana[1]	7,500	30	Yes	No
Nebraska	25,000	30	Yes	No

Nevada	10,000	30	Yes	No
New Hampshire[2,7]	500	0	Yes	No
New Jersey[2,3]	10,000	0	No	No
New Mexico[1]	20,000	30	Yes	No
New York	10,000	30	Yes	No
North Carolina	20,000	30	Yes	Yes
North Dakota[1]	15,000	30	Yes	No
Ohio[7]	2,500	0	Yes	No
Oklahoma	Not Available			
Oregon	60,000	30	No	Yes
Pennsylvania	Not Available			
Rhode Island[1]	7,500	45	Yes	No[6]
South Carolina[1]	10,000	30	Yes	No
South Dakota	25,000	0	Yes	Yes
Tennessee	1,000	30	Yes	No
Texas	50,000	30	Yes	No
Utah[1]	25,000	30	Yes	No
Vermont	Not Available			
Virginia	10,000	60	Yes	No
Washington[1]	60,000	40	Yes	Yes
West Virginia[7]	1,000	120	Yes	No
Wisconsin	10,000	0	Yes	No
Wyoming[1]	70,000	30	Yes	Yes

[1] Not available if petition for appointment of personal representative has been granted or is pending.
[2] Available only if deceased is survived by a spouse.
[3] Available only if deceased left no will.
[4] Not more than two vehicles plus a boat (maximum value of $5,000) plus life insurance (maximum value of $1000).
[5] Life insurance up to $2,000 plus bank accounts up to $3,000 and wages up to $100.
[6] Funeral expenses must first be paid.
[7] Available only for wages, salaries, and commissions.

□ Transfer by Summary Probate Administration.

Summary probate administration is available in two forms, one for very small estates ($2,500, for example), the other for estates of higher value. The procedure for very small estates is quite simple and usually does not require the appointment of a personal representative, notice to creditors, a final accounting, or any of the other formalities required by formal probate administration.

Under this procedure, any survivor interested in the deceased's estate files with the probate court a petition, along with proof that the funeral bill has been paid. The court clerk or judge then signs an order transferring all of the deceased's property to the person(s) designated by the petitioner as being entitled by law to receive the assets. This form of transfer procedure may include real estate, but since the dollar limit is low, it is unlikely it can be used effectively for the transfer of real property.

The second type of summary probate administration has a limit in some states of $60,000 or more. Thus, it may be used effectively to transfer real estate as well as personal property.

Under this procedure, a surviving interested person files a petition with the probate court, which then appoints a personal representative. Unlike the personal representative appointed for full probate administration, this one may not have to be bonded and may not be required to make a full inventory of assets, notify the deceased's creditors, or submit an accounting to the court. His or her sole responsibility, after submitting proof that the funeral bill has been paid, is to transfer all of the deceased's assets to the persons specified in the deceased's will or, if there was no will, to the deceased's state-specified heirs at law. Depending on state law, these assets may or may not be subject to the claims of creditors.

The procedures described here, which can often be accomplished in a few days, are embodied in the Uniform Probate Code. And most of the 35 states that have not adopted the code have similar small-estate transfer procedures. Details and forms are available from the local probate court.

State Requirements For Small Estate Summary Probate Procedure

State	Dollar Limitation ($)	Waiting Period Following Death	Procedure Excludes Real Estate	Creditors Must First Be Paid
Alabama	3,000	No	Yes	Yes
Alaska	Formula[2]	No	No	No
Arizona	Formula[2]	No	No	No
Arkansas	Formula[3]	No	Yes	No
California	60,000	No	No	No
Colorado	Formula[2]	No	No	No
Connecticut	Not Available			
Delaware	Not Available			
DC	15,000	No	No	No
Florida	60,000	No	No	Yes
Georgia	Unlimited	No	No	Yes
Hawaii	20,000	No	No	No
Idaho	Formula[2]	No	No	No
Illinois5	50,000[4]	No	No	Yes
Indiana	Formula[2]	No	No	No
Iowa[6]	50,000	No	No	Yes
Kansas	Formula[2]	6 months	No	Yes
Kentucky[5,7]	7,500	No	No	Yes
Louisiana	Not Available			
Maine	Formula2	No	No	No
Maryland	20,000	30 days	Yes	Yes
Massachusetts[1]	15,000	30 days	Yes	No
Michigan	Formula2	No	No	No
Minnesota1,[8]	30,000	No	No	No
Mississippi	Not Available			
Missouri	Formula[2]	No	No	No
Montana	Formula[2]	No	No	No
Nebraska	Formula[2]	No	No	No
Nevada	100,000	60 days	No	Yes
New Hampsire	5,000	No	No	Yes
New Jersey[7,8]	10,000	No	No	No
New Mexico	Formula2	No	No	Yes
New York[8]	Unlimited	No	No	No
North Carolina[7]	Unlimited	No	No	No
North Dakota	Unlimited	No	No	No
Ohio	35,000	No	No	Yes
Oklahoma	60,000	No	No	Yes
Oregon	140,000	No	No	Yes
Pennsylvania	10,000	No	Yes	No
Rhode Island	Not Available			
South Carolina[8]	10,000	No	No	No
South Dakota	60,000	No	No	Yes
Tennessee	10,000	45 days	No	Yes
Texas	Formula[2]	No	No	Yes
Utah	Formula[2]	No	No	No
Vermont	10,000	No	Yes	Yes

Virginia	10,000	60 days	Yes	No
Washington	Not Available			
West Virginia	50,000	No	No	No
Wisconsin	30,000	No	No	Yes
Wyoming	70,000	No	No	Yes

[1] Not available if petition for appointment of personal representative has been granted or is pending.
[2] Available where entire estate, less liens and encumbrances, does not exceed certain statutory allowances plus expenses of last illness, funeral, and administration.
[3] If personal property is less than statutory dower and allowances to widow or minors, court may immediately assign estate to them.
[4] Includes deceased's probate and nonprobate assets.
[5] Available only if all beneficiaries consent in writing.
[6] Available only if deceased is survived by a spouse, children, or a parent.
[7] Available only if deceased is survived by a spouse.
[8] Available only if deceased left no will.
[9] Exclusive of statutory family allowances or exempt property.

FORMAL PROBATE ADMINISTRATION ■

If you are not eligible to use the small-estate transfer procedures described above, and if the deceased's probate assets do not amount to more than a few hundred dollars, you may decide to simply abandon the assets. If these assets are substantial, though, survivors will have no choice but to commence formal probate administration.

Depending on the complexity of the deceased's estate and the skill of the personal representative, formal probate can take anywhere from a few months to several years. Moreover, it can be expensive. The personal representative is entitled to be paid for his or her services and to be reimbursed for all expenses. In addition, court costs and fees for lawyers, accountants, and appraisers must be paid by the estate before it can be closed.

The basic process of probate administration can help to explain why it is lengthy and costly. First, a personal representative must be appointed by the court to collect, manage, and settle the deceased's probate assets. The court must determine the validity of the deceased's will. The personal representative must identify and notify all beneficiaries named in the will and all heirs at law (those designated by state law to inherit if there is no will). The personal representative must also notify the deceased's known creditors, invite them to submit claims, and determine the legitimacy of these claims. After all claims and taxes have been paid, the personal representative must submit a final accounting to the court and then distribute any remaining assets to the entitled beneficiaries

Even if the deceased's will has previously been filed with the local probate court for safekeeping, probate administration does not begin automatically upon the testator's death. To initiate probate administration, an "interested party" must petition the court to appoint a personal representative and commence probate administration. If the deceased's assets are substantial and there is no will or the will failed to name a personal representative who is available and willing to act, there will be no dearth of interested parties. Beneficiaries or heirs will be eager to inherit the deceased's assets, and creditors will want to collect on unpaid debts.

Because the deceased's probate assets can be collected, managed, and transferred to survivors only by a personal representative, his or her appointment by the court is the first order of business.

If you have been named in the will as personal representative, you may feel daunted by the responsibilities that confront you. Bear in mind, however, that you have the right to hire lawyers, accountants, and other professionals, and that their fees are payable with estate funds. In addition, you are entitled to reasonable compensation for your services, plus reimbursement for your expenses.

You can, of course, decline to serve as personal representative, in which case the court will appoint a substitute, usually an adult beneficiary named in the will, another heir at law if there is no will, or a creditor of the estate. If none of these people is willing to petition for the appointment, the court may appoint a bank, a trust company, a lawyer (sometimes a political friend), or any other person or entity.

Your decision to undertake the responsibility, then, may depend on your status as a beneficiary and your relationship to other survivors. If you are concerned with conserving the probate assets, you are likely, despite your "amateur" standing, to do a more conscientious job than a bank or other professional taking the job solely for financial gain.

If you decide to serve, your first step is to retain a lawyer, preferably one specializing in probate, to prepare and file a petition requesting your formal appointment and the commencement of probate proceedings. Once the petition is granted, the probate court will formalize your appointment and issue you letters of authority, the document that authorizes you to act on behalf of the estate, including the management and ultimate distribution of the deceased's probate assets.

The Personal Representative □

Once appointed, the personal representative has much the same power over probate assets as the deceased had over those assets during his or her lifetime. Armed with the letters of authority, the personal representative may sell assets owned by the estate, manage an existing business, make investments with estate funds, mortgage estate property, and do anything else necessary to preserve or increase the value of the estate. In brief, he may be regarded as the deceased's alter ego, empowered to manage all of the deceased's financial affairs.

The personal representative's activities are, however, subject to three limitations. First, unlike the deceased, who could do absolutely whatever he wished with his property, the personal representative must act "prudently," so as not to jeopardize the value of the estate. Second, he must do everything he can to settle the estate as promptly as possible. Third, he must do nothing with respect to the estate that works to his personal advantage, such as buying for himself an estate asset at an unreasonably low price.

In some states, the personal representative's compensation is specified as a percentage of the value of the estate. In California, for example, the personal representative is entitled to receive as compensation 4% of the first $15,000 of estate assets, 3% of the next $85,000, 2% of the next $900,000, 1% of the next $900,000, and 1/2% of the next $15 million. When the fee is not established by law, a personal representative's compensation is expected to be "reasonable," and is subject to challenge in the probate court by any interested party—beneficiary, heir, or creditor.

If you are a beneficiary of the estate as well as the personal representative, you may prefer to waive your fee so as to preserve the value of the estate, particularly since your fee is taxable as ordinary income, whereas your inheritance is not.

The deceased's will may specify that the personal representative is to serve without bond. If this is not specified, the estate is charged the cost of bond premiums. The purpose of the bond is to protect all interested parties against fraud, negligence, or embezzlement on the part of the personal representative in managing and disposing of the estate's assets. Typically, annual bond premiums are based on the total value of the estate, costing about $5 per $1,000 of probatable assets.

If the will specifies that the personal representative may serve without bond, the probate judge may override this provision and require bonding if he or she believes it necessary for the protection of beneficiaries or creditors. Conversely, if the will does not address bonding and if the personal representative is the sole beneficiary, the judge may waive the bond requirement.

Bonding is easily arranged through almost any insurance agent, but, despite the pressure of time, shopping around is advisable. If the value of the estate's assets is substantial, the personal representative can sometimes negotiate a discount on the premium from an insurance agent eager to sell this coverage.

Because bond premiums are payable annually and renewed automatically until the estate is settled, the personal representative should cancel the bond as soon as the estate is closed by sending the insurance company a copy of the court's "Order Closing the Estate and Discharging the Personal Representative." The personal representative should also request a refund of unearned premiums.

□ "Proving" the Will

The initial petition for appointment of a personal representative typically includes a request that the court approve the deceased's will or, if there is no will, determine which of the heirs at law listed in the petition are entitled to inherit the estate's assets. In response, the court schedules a hearing and sends a notification of its time and place to all interested parties—creditors, beneficiaries named in the will, and heirs at law. At this hearing, the will may be contested by any interested party.

□ Will Contests

Will contests are a rare event, and only a very small percentage are successful. The party contesting the will must have a direct interest in the estate. In other words, he or she must stand to gain if the contest is successful. Thus, all heirs-at-law—persons who would have inherited had there been no will—have the right to contest the will. A child or other heir-at-law specifically disinherited in the will also has "standing" to contest it. In addition, a non-heir-at-law not mentioned in the will may contest it if he or she is a beneficiary named in a previous will. However, a divorced spouse has no right to contest a will even if he or she was mentioned in a previous will. A stepchild has no right of inheritance under state intestacy laws, but, like other non-heirs-at-law, may contest the will if he or she is a beneficiary mentioned in a previous will. Although ex-spouses have no right to contest their former partner's will, this may not deter them from threatening to initiate a contest in the hope that the personal representative will offer a settlement rather than pay the costs of defending against a will contest.

Grounds for Contesting a Will

A will can be contested on any of the following grounds:

- Lack of testamentary capacity

    Evidence that the testator was not "of sound mind" when he or she signed the will is grounds for setting aside the will. But such evidence is difficult to establish. Eccentricity, or even periods of incompetence, may not constitute good grounds since even eccentrics and the mentally disturbed are known to have moments of lucidity. In cases of Alzheimer's and AIDS, courts have ruled against will contestants, noting neither illness, by itself, is conclusive evidence of diminished capacity.

    If the will was signed in the presence of a lawyer, the lawyer is likely to have ascertained the testator's mental condition through conversation on a variety of subjects. And in some cases involving large estates, the signing is recorded on videotape. When a contest appears likely, a prudent lawyer will obtain written statements from physicians and nurses familiar with the testator, attesting to the individual's soundness of mind at the time of signing. Your lawyer will also do well to choose witnesses to the signing who are likely to be alive and consequently available to testify if the will is contested.

- Improper execution

    Technical errors—in witnessing, dating, or any

other omission or departure from the legal requirements—are somewhat easier to demonstrate than incapacity, and even a seemingly trivial error may inval-
idate a will. Self-made wills are especially vulnerable
to contest on such grounds.

- Undue influence

    Persons omitted from the will or those who have
received less than another beneficiary may feel the
testator was subject to the undue influence of another beneficiary, especially if the provisions of the most
recent will differ radically from those of an earlier
will. Claims of undue influence may also be made by
children, parents, or siblings who have been disinherited in favor of a gay or lesbian domestic partner.
Such claims are difficult to prove since the alleged influence probably did not occur in the presence of witnesses. If undue influence is proved, however, the
will can be set aside.

- Fraud or mistake

    Many will contestants who allege undue influence
are likely to allege fraud as well. Fraud occurs when a
testator has been deceived as to the contents of his will
or other facts that relate to the disposition of his property. A mistake results in the same outcome as fraud
but does not involve the knowing participation of another person. In either case, the court will rule the testator acted on false information. Wills are readily set
aside when fraud is proven but rarely invalidated as a
result of mistake.

- Revocation

    If the contesting party can produce a valid will executed later in time that expressly revokes the will offered by the personal representative, the more recent will is likely to be admitted and the earlier will rejected.
- Bogus will

    A purported will proven not to have been executed by the testator will be invalidated.

The Process of Contesting a Will □

Once a contestant with standing decides to contest the will, he or she will probably retain an attorney experienced in probate law to set the contest in motion by informing the court of the contestant's objections to the offered will. Because at this point probate proceedings can come to a complete halt, there may be pressure on the personal representative to offer a "nuisance" settlement, as other beneficiaries may be eager to close the estate and receive their inheritances.

In recent years, courts have become unsympathetic to frivolous will contests, and often require unsuccessful contestants to pay costs and legal fees incurred by both parties.

If a will is successfully contested, the court will decline to "admit" the will to probate. In such case, the deceased will be regarded as having died intestate unless there is an earlier valid will available to be admitted to probate.

If the will is not successfully contested, the court will admit it to probate, with the terms of the admitted will governing the subsequent probate proceedings.

☐ Notification of Interested Parties

Once appointed, the personal representative must send each interested party (beneficiaries, heirs-at-law, and creditors) written notification of his or her appointment, including his or her name and address, and the location of the probate court where the will and other documents relating to the estate are filed. This notice informs interested parties about the personal representative's appointment and offers an opportunity to challenge the will. In addition, the notice invites the interested parties to ascertain the value of the estate by consulting an inventory, filed by the personal representative with the probate court, listing the current value of each of the estate's assets as well as any mortgages or liens against the assets. By examining this inventory, beneficiaries and/or heirs-at-law can estimate what they may expect to inherit, and creditors can determine whether they are likely to collect all or part of their debts.

☐ Dealing with Creditors

Upon appointment, the personal representative must send written notice to each of the deceased's known creditors inviting them to submit, in writing and within a specified time limit, all claims they have against the estate. In addition, the personal representative must publish the notice in a newspaper circulated in the county in which the deceased lived to inform creditors of whom the personal representative is not aware. The number and timing of the notice to creditors and the period of time during which creditors may respond are governed by state law. Typically, the creditor must submit a written claim to the personal representative and also file a copy with the court. In all states, claims submitted after the deadline will be barred as untimely and need not be paid.

The personal representative must pay legitimate claims in the order in which he or she receives them, unless the possibility exists that the estate's assets will not cover all taxes and claims. In such case, taxes and claims must be paid according to the priority established by state law, typically as follows:

1) Costs of administering the estate, including the personal representative's fees, expenses, and bond premiums, lawyers' and other professionals' fees, and court costs

2) Reasonable funeral expenses and medical bills incurred by the deceased

3) Taxes and whatever debts state law specifies as having priority, and

4) All other legitimate debts

Under this priority system, high-priority creditors are paid in full and, if no assets remain, low-priority creditors get nothing. If, after paying all claims in priorities 1, 2, and 3, the estate remains with $500 in assets and $1,000 in debts, each Class 4 creditor will receive 50% of his or her claim.

TAXES—FEDERAL AND STATE ■

Income Taxes □

The personal representative is responsible for preparing

and filing the deceased's income tax returns—federal, state, and local. This duty extends to the estate if the estate earned more than $600 during any year, possibly from the operation of a business, or yield on bank accounts, investments, and loans. Even if the deceased died on January 1, tax returns may be due for that year.

□ Federal Gift and Estate Tax

The personal representative is responsible for paying any federal gift and estate tax. At the time of this writing the federal government levies this tax on all estates valued at more than $650,000. The 1997 Taxpayer Relief Act increased this exemption, in annual stages, to $1 million in 2006.

If this figure strikes you as too high to be applicable to your situation, you may be tempted to skip the remainder of this section. Before doing so, however, bear in mind that the values of both real estate and securities have escalated in recent years. In addition, if there is a wrongful-death claim pending, its settlement could raise the value of the taxable estate above the $650,000 minimum. The value of the taxable estate may also be significantly increased by life insurance proceeds, retirement accounts, and part or all of the value of jointly owned assets.

With respect to this federal death tax, gay and lesbian domestic partners suffer a distinct disadvantage as compared to legally married couples. Under the "Unlimited Marital Deduction," embodied in the federal gift and estate tax, surviving spouses who are U.S. citizens can inherit an unlimited amount from a deceased spouse without payment of any federal estate tax. Unless the surviving spouse remarries, though, that individual's estate in excess of $650,000 will be subject to the federal gift and estate tax on his or her subsequent death. No such marital deduction is available to a surviving gay or lesbian domestic partner.

Basically, the unified gift and estate tax offers everyone a $650,000 exemption. This can best be understood if you regard it as a lifetime "line of credit." Against this line of credit must be charged any gift of more than $3,000 made before 1982, plus any subsequent gift of more than $10,000, plus the value of the deceased's taxable estate at the time of the death.

Thus, if while alive and after 1982 the deceased made three annual gifts of $15,000 each, and his or her taxable estate is worth $545,000 upon his or her death in 1998, the total "charges" against his or her $625,000 exemption would be $590,000. Thus, the deceased's estate would not be subject to estate tax.

In calculating the value of a deceased's taxable estate, it is important to note that it may include nonprobate as well as probate assets. The taxable estate includes solely owned assets and all other assets in which the deceased had an interest at the time of death, including jointly owned assets, life insurance proceeds, assets held in the deceased's revocable living trust, IRA, 401(k), and Keogh retirement accounts, gifts of life insurance made within three years of death, custodial accounts for minors for which the deceased was the donor if the deceased was serving as custodian at the time of death, and the deceased's partial interest in any community property.

For purposes of computing the federal gift and estate tax,

the total value of the deceased's assets can be determined either as of the date of death or six months after death.

The estate tax return (IRS Form 706) is due nine months after the date of death. It is the personal representative's responsibility to file the return and pay any tax due. If it is impossible or impracticable for you to file within this time limit, the IRS may grant an extension, usually no more than six months, but this extension does not allow you to postpone payment of the tax when it is due. Thus, any application for filing time extension must be accompanied by payment of the estimated tax.

Because it is likely the value of the estate you are administering does not exceed the $650,000 minimum, we will not provide complete instructions for calculating the tax and filing a return. If the estate is subject to federal gift and estate tax, you should contact an experienced tax lawyer and/or accountant. A relatively simple formula by which you can determine whether the estate is likely to be subject to the tax is:

(value of the gross estate) - (deductions) = (adjusted gross estate) - (charitable gifts) = (taxable estate)

To determine the value of the gross estate, add the value of all assets that are subject to federal estate tax. Then add the total value of gifts exceeding $10,000 that the deceased made during his or her lifetime. This total represents the value of the gross estate.

Deductions that may be subtracted from the gross estate

consist of hospital and medical expenses incurred by the deceased during his or her final illness, funeral and burial expenses, estate administration expenses (including the personal representative's expenses and compensation, bond premiums, probate court costs, and legal and other professional fees), and the deceased's debts, mortgages, and other liabilities. Subtracting the deductions from the gross estate determines the adjusted gross estate.

From the adjusted gross estate you may then deduct all bequests to charitable and other eligible nonprofit organizations. The result is the value of the deceased's taxable estate.

Federal Estate Taxes

In the case of estates of decedents dying and gifts made during:	Applicable exclusion amount	Applicable credit amount (based upon current tax rate schedule)
1998	$ 625,000	$ 202,050
1999	$ 650,000	$ 211,300
2000 and 2001	$ 675,000	$ 220,550
2002 and 2003	$ 700,000	$ 229,800
2004	$ 850,000	$ 287,300
2005	$ 950,000	$ 326,300
2006 or thereafter	$ 1,000,000	$ 345,800

If the taxable value of the estate does not exceed the values shown in the table above, you need do nothing. If it does, you should seek professional help. If federal estate tax is due, the probate court will not permit the distribution of bequests and closure of the estate until the personal representative produces a tax clearance letter from the Internal Revenue Service.

□ State Death Taxes

Most states impose one of two kinds of death taxes. The first is an estate tax, payable by the estate. The second is an inheritance or succession tax, payable by the beneficiaries.

In some states the estate tax is simply a percentage of the federal estate tax. In those states an estate exempt from the federal estate tax will also be exempt from state estate tax.

State Inheritance Tax Rates and Exemptions, as of December 31, 1996

	Rate Percent		
State	Spouse, Child or Parent	Brother or Sister	Other than Relative
Connecticut	2-8	4-10	8-14
Delaware	2-4	5-10	10-16
Indiana	1-10	7-15	10-20
Iowa	1-8	5-10	10-15
Kansas	1-5	3-12.5	10-15
Kentucky	2-10	2-10	6-16
Louisiana	2-3	5-7	5-10
Maryland	1	10	10
Montana	2-8	4-16	8-32
Nebraska	1	1	6-18
New Hampshire	1	18	18
New Jersey	Exempt	11-16	15-16
North Carolina	1-12	4-16	8-17
Pennsylvania	6	15	15
South Dakota	3-15	4-20	6-30
Tennessee	5.5-9.5	5.5-9.5	5.5-9.5
Texas	(d)	(d)	(d)

(a) For all others, the exemption is the greater of the statutory amount of (1) one-fourth of each beneficiary's interest, if the decedent dies between July 1, 1995, and June 30, 1996; (2) one-half of each beneficiary's interest, if the decedent dies between July 1, 1996, and June 30, 1997; (3) three-fourths of each beneficiary's interest, if the decedent dies between July 1, 1997, and June 30, 1998; or (4) each beneficiary's total inheritable interest, if the decedent dies after June 30, 1998.

(b) No tax on transfers of real property and first $100,000 of property other than real property.

Other states are considerably less liberal, but provide exemptions of various kinds.

Although inheritance taxes are payable by the beneficiary, the deceased's will may specify that the tax is to be paid by the estate on behalf of the beneficiaries. In any event, it is the responsibility of the personal representative to make sure the tax is paid, because the probate court will normally insist on a tax clearance certificate issued by the state treasurer's office before signing an order discharging the personal representative and closing the estate.

| | Exemptions (Thousands of dollars) | | |
Spouse	Child/ Parent	Brother or Sister	Other than Relative
All	50	6	1
70	25	5	1
All	5/10	0.5	0.1
All	50/15	None	None
All	30	5	None
All	(a)	(a)	0.5
25	25	1	0.5
(b)	(b)	0.15	0.15
All	All/7	1	None
All	10	2	0.5
All	All	None	None
All	All	25	0.5
All	26.15 credit	None	None
(c)	2	None	None
All	30	0.5	0.1
600	600	600	600
(d)	(d)	(d)	(d)

(c) For a surviving spouse, the rate is 3% for estates of decedents dying on or after January 1, 1998.
(d) the amount due is the portion of the federal credit attributable to property in Texas. Only estates that have federal estate tax liabilities are subject to the inheritance tax. Note: In addition to an inheritance tax, all states listed also levy an estate tax, generally to assure full absorption of the federal credit.
Source: Commerce Clearing House and respective state revenue departments.

State Estate Tax Rates and Exemptions, as of December 31, 1996

State (a)	Rates (On Net Estate After Exemptions) (b)	Maximum Rate Applies Above	Exemption
Alabama	Maximum Federal credit (c),(d)	$10,040,000	$60,000 (c)
Alaska	Maximum Federal credit (c),(d)	$10,040,000	$60,000 (c)
Arizona	Maximum Federal credit (c),(d)	$10,040,000	$60,000 (c)
Arkansas	Maximum Federal credit (c),(d)	$10,040,000	$60,000 (c)
California	Maximum Federal credit (c),(d)	$10,040,000	$60,000 (c)
Colorado	Maximum Federal credit (c),(d)	$10,040,000	$60,000 (c)
Florida	Maximum Federal credit (c),(d)	$10,040,000	$60,000 (c)
Georgia	Maximum Federal credit (c),(d)	$10,040,000	$60,000 (c)
Hawaii	Maximum Federal credit (c),(d)	$10,040,000	$60,000 (c)
Idaho	Maximum Federal credit (c),(d)	$10,040,000	$60,000 (c)
Illinois	Maximum Federal credit (c),(d)	$10,040,000	$60,000 (c)
Maine	Maximum Federal credit (c),(d)	$10,040,000	$60,000 (c)
Massachusetts	5% on first $60,000 to 16%	$4,000,000	$600,000
Michigan	Maximum Federal credit (c),(d)	$10,040,000	$60,000
Minnesota	Maximum Federal credit (c),(d)	$10,040,000	$60,000
Mississippi	1% on first $60,000 to 16%	$10,000,000	$600,000
Missouri	Maxium Federal credit	$10,040,000	$60,000 (c)
Nevada	Maximimum Federal credit (c),(d)	$10,040,000	$60,000 (c)
New Mexico	Maximum Federal credit (c),(d)	$10,040,000	$60,000 (c)
New York	2% on first $50,0000 to 21%	$10,100,000	Varies
North Dakota	Maximum Federal Credit (c),(d)	$10,040,000	$60,000 (c)
Ohio	2% on first $40,000 to 7%	$500,000	$10,000 (e)
Oklahoma	0.5% on first $10,000 to 10% (f)	$10,000,000	(g)
Oregon	Maximum Federal Credit (c),(d)	$1,000,000	$25,000 (h)
Rhode Island	2% on First $25,000 to 9%	$10,040,000	$60,000 (c)
South Carolina	Maximum Federal Credit (c),(d)	$10,040,000	$60,000 (c)
Utah	Maximum Federal Credit (c),(d)	$10,040,000	$60,000 (c)
Vermont	Maximum Federal Credit (c),(d)	$10,040,000	$60,000 (c)
Virginia	Maximum Federal Credit (c),(d)	$10,040,000	$60,000 (c)
Washington	Maximum Federal Credit (c),(d)	$10,040,000	$60,000 (c)
West Virginia	Maximum Federal Credit (c),(d)	$10,040,000	$60,000 (c)

Wisconsin	Maximum Federal Credit (c),(d)	$10,040,000	$60,000 (c)
Wyoming	Maximum Federal Credit (c),(d)	$10,040,000	$60,000 (c)
DC	Maximum Federal Credit (c),(d)	$10,040,000	$60,000 (c)

(a) Excludes states shown in inheritance tax table.
(b) The rates generally are in addition to graduated absolute amounts.
(c) Maximum federal credit allowed under the 1954 Code for state estate taxes paid is expressed as a percentage of the taxable estate (after $60,000 exemption) in excess of $40,000, plus a graduated absolute amount. The $60,000 exemption is allowed uder the State Death Tax Credit.
(d) A tax on nonresident estates is imposed on the proportionate share of the estate which the property located in the state bears to the entire estate wherever situated.
(e) A credit equal to the lesser of $500 or the amount of the estate is allowed. A marital deduction is allowed in an amount equal to the net value of any asset passing from the decedent to the receiving spouse, but only to the extent that the asset is included in the value of the Ohio gross estate.
(f) Rates apply only to lineal heirs. For collateral heirs the rates vary from 1% on the first 10,000 to 15% on amounts of $1 million or more.
(g) Exemption is a total aggregate of $175,000 for father, mother, child, and named relatives. Property passing to surviving spouse is entirely excluded.
(h) Marital deduction is $175,000.
Source: Commerce Clearing House and respective state revenue departments.

DISTRIBUTING THE ESTATE ■

Once all debts, taxes, and other liabilities of the estate have been fully paid, the personal representative is ready to distribute the remaining probate assets to the entitled beneficiaries and to submit to the court a final accounting of his or her actions.

Modifications to the distribution specified by the will or by state law if there is no will can be achieved if all beneficiaries give written consent. For example, a parent who is a beneficiary can ask that his or her share be distributed equally to his or her surviving children, even though the children were not mentioned in the will. Such a request, however, might not relieve the original beneficiary of inheritance tax liability.

If one or more of the beneficiaries is a minor and the value of his or her bequest is not large, the distribution can often be made directly to his or her parent or guardian. If the amount is substantial—usually over $5,000—it must be paid to the minor's conservator or guardian as appointed by the probate court.

In distributing the assets, it is prudent for the personal representative to protect himself by obtaining a receipt from each beneficiary to avoid future claims. As soon as the personal representative has completed distribution, he or she prepares for signature by the probate court an order allowing the final account and assigning the residue to the beneficiaries. Once it has been signed, the order serves as a formal record indicating when, how, and to whom the estate's assets were distributed.

■ CLOSING THE ESTATE

After distribution of the estate's assets, the personal representative files with the court a closing statement certifying he or she has paid all claims and taxes, and distributed the residue in accordance with the will or with state law if there was no will. The personal representative then sends a copy of the closing statement to all interested parties. Upon approval of the closing statement, the probate court issues to the personal representative an order discharging him or her from his or her position and any further responsibilities. At this point the estate is closed.

SAMPLE FORMS

The forms shown in this chapter are intended for your general information and not for your actual use, because some of them require more than just filling in the blanks. Your own will, for example, is likely to be far more complicated than the model shown here and may require the help of a lawyer to make certain it complies with the laws of your state.

Examining these forms, however, will give you a clear idea of their purpose and their complexity.

AFFIDAVIT FOR COLLECTION OF PERSONAL PROPERTY
(Minn. Statutes 524.3-1201)

I, the undersigned, state as follows:

1._____, the decedent, died on

_____.

2. The value of the entire probate estate, wherever located, including specifically any contents of a safe deposit box, less liens and encumbrances, does not exceed $20,000.

3. At least thirty days have elapsed since the decedent's death, as shown by the attached certified copy of the decedent's death certificate.

4. No application or petition for the appointment of a personal representative is pending or has been granted in any jurisdiction.

5. I, the undersigned, am entitled to payment or delivery, under the terms of the decedent's will, of the following property.

_____

_____

_____

6. I declare that the foregoing is true and correct.

_____   _____

Date   Signature

.... [notarization]

WILL

LAST WILL AND TESTAMENT OF

I,   domiciled in Lansing, Michigan, declare this to be
my last will, hereby revoking all previous wills and codicils.

FIRST

1.1 *Payments of Debts and Taxes:* I direct my Personal Representative
to pay all of my legally enforceable debts, expenses of last illness, funeral and burial expenses, and expenses of administering my estate. I
direct my Personal Representative to pay all taxes imposed by reason of
my death upon any transfer of property includable in my estate, as an
expense of administration, unless voluntarily paid by some party.

SECOND

2.1 *Specific Bequest:* I give and bequeath my stamp collection to my
son,   , if he survives me; otherwise this gift shall lapse.

2.2 *Disposition of Residue:* I give, devise, and bequeath all of the rest,
residue, and remainder of my estate, real, personal or mixed, wherever
situate and whether acquired before or after the execution of this will, to
(hereafter "my lifetime partner"), if he/she survives me.

2.3 *Alternative disposition—Residue:* If my lifetime partner does not
survive me, then I give, devise, and bequeath all of the said remainder of
my estate to my children surviving me, in equal shares, provided, however, the issue of a deceased child surviving me shall take and share
equally the share that their parent would have taken had he or she survived me. If my issue do not agree to this division among them, the decision of my Personal Representative shall be in all respects binding upon
my issue.

THIRD

3.1 *Survivorship Defined:* In the event that my lifetime partner and I
die under circumstances where it cannot be established who died first,
then it shall be presumed that my lifetime partner survived me and this
will and the dispositions hereunder shall be construed on that presump-
tion. No person other than my lifetime partner shall be deemed to have
survived me or to be living at my death if he or she shall die within
ninety (90) days after my death.

FOURTH

4.1 *Personal Representative:* I nominate my lifetime partner as my
Personal Representative, to serve without bond. If my lifetime partner
predeceases me, declines to act, or having qualified, resigns, dies, or is
removed, I nominate Capitol Bank and Trust Company, Lansing, Michigan, as my Personal Representative.

WILL

4.2 *Powers:* I give my Personal Representative all powers of administration granted to independent personal representatives as set forth in the Michigan Revised Probate Code at the time of execution of this will, including the power to sell any real or personal property, and for that purpose I hereby incorporate those powers by reference.

4.3 *Guardian and Conservator:* In the event that my lifetime partner fails to survive me, I nominate and appoint my brother and his wife, _____ and _____ , Cleveland, Ohio, as Guardians of the person and Capitol Bank and Trust Company, Lansing, Michigan, as Conservator of the estate, of any of my children who is a minor at the time of my death.

_____

On _____ , the above testator signed the foregoing instrument (typewritten on two [2] sheets of paper, upon the bottom of each of which he/she also signed) and declared that he/she signed it freely and voluntarily as his/her Last Will; we witnessed the signing in the presence of said testator, and we now, on the same day, sign as witnesses in the presence of said testator and of each other; to the best of our knowledge, said testator is now 18 or more years of age, of sound mind, and under no constraint or undue influence.

Witnesses: Addresses:

_____   _____

_____   _____

CODICIL

FIRST CODICIL TO LAST WILL OF

I,   declare this to be the First Codicil to my Last Will dated

I hereby revoke in their entirety Items 2.1 and 4.3 of my Last Will dated   and substitute in lieu thereof new Items with the same numbers, which Items shall read as follows:

2.1 *Specific Bequest:* I give and bequeath my stamp collection to my daughter, SALLY L. JONES, if she survives me; otherwise this gift shall lapse.

4.3 *Guardian and Conservator:* In the event that my lifetime partner fails to survive me, I nominate and appoint my friend,   and his wife,   as Guardians of the person and Liberty Federal Bank, Lansing, Michigan, as Conservator of the estate of any of my children who is a minor at the time of my death.

SECOND

I republish and reaffirm my said Last Will as herein modified, amended, and supplemented by this First Codicil as if the same were set out here in full and do incorporate the same by this reference thereto.

_____

On   , the above person signed the foregoing instrument (typewritten on one [1] sheet of paper) and declared that he/she signed it freely and voluntarily as the First Codicil to his/her Last Will; we witnessed the signing in the presence of said person, and we now, on the same day, sign as witnesses in the presence of said person and of each other; to the best of our knowledge, said person is now 18 or more years of age, of sound mind, and under no constraint or undue influence.

Witnesses: Addresses:

_____   _____

_____   _____

HOLOGRAPHIC WILL

Will of John J. Jones

I, John J. Jones, declare this to be my last will. I revoke all prior wills.

First: I leave my art collection to my son, William B. Jones.

Second: I leave the rest of my property to my life partner, Robert R. Roe, if he survives me. If he does not survive me, I leave the rest of my property to my children, in equal shares. If any of my children die before me, then that child's share shall go to that child's children by right of representation.

Third: If it cannot be determined if I or my life partner died first, then it shall be presumed that I survived my life partner.

Fourth: I nominate my life partner as Personal Representative. If he does not act, I nominate my son William in his place. My Representative need not post bond.

Fifth: If my children need a guardian, I nominate my brother, Richard J. Jones.

Dated: January 15, 1997

John J. Jones

PERSONAL PROPERTY ASSIGNMENT

The undersigned   and   (Assignors), whose
address is   hereby assign, grant, and
transfer to   and   as joint tenants with
rights of survivorship, all of Assignors' right, title, and interest in and to
the following described personal property:

(a) All of the household furnishing, appliances, equipment, tools, books, collectibles, artwork, and all other items of tangible personal property now and hereafter located at or contained in Assignor's dwelling at   , and any other dwelling occupied by Assignors; and

(b) All of the contents now and hereafter contained in Assignors' safe deposit box at First of America Bank, and any other safe deposit box leased to Assignors or either of them.

Assignors:

Date: _____   _____

_____

REAL ESTATE DEED

KNOW ALL MEN BY THESE PRESENTS: That
whose address is
Quit Claim(s) to
whose address is
the following described premises situated in the   of
                County of   and State of Michigan, to-wit:

for the full consideration of

Dated this   day of   19
     Witnesses: Signed and Sealed:
_____   _____ (L.S.)
_____   _____ (L.S.)
                                 _____ (L.S.)
STATE OF MICHIGAN } SS.
COUNTY OF   _____ (L.S.)

The foregoing instrument was acknowledged before me this
day of   19 by
   My commission expires _____

_____ Notary Public _____ County, Michigan

Prepared by:
_____

_____   _____
=========================   ==========================

Recording Fee _____   When recorded return to _____
State Transfer Tax _____   _____
                            Send subsequent tax bills
                            to _____
Tax Parcel # _____   _____

REVOCABLE LIVING TRUST

DECLARATION OF TRUST made on the date set forth below
by   and   ,
hereafter called "Trustees", with reference to the following facts:

(a)   and   are lifetime partners
and hold title to all of their property as joint tenants;

(b)   and   are their only
children; each of them has children;

(c)   and   would like to avoid
probate, not only in the event of the death of disability of one of them,
but also on the death of the survivor of them, but want assurance that,
in the event of the disability of one or both of them, property will be
applied toward his, her or their care and, upon the death of the survivor
of them, will be distributed to their issue who survive such survivor,
per stirpes;

(d) The parties have decided upon holding such property in joint
tenancy, with full rights of survivorship, and without any mention of a
trust on the record, but with a declaration and acknowledgment that
those who succeed, or the one who succeeds, to the title on the death or
disability of another or others are, or is, actually holding as trustees, or
trustee, for the purposes and on the conditions hereinafter set forth.

THE PARTIES AGREE:

1. ESTABLISHMENT OF TRUST. Any property assigned, hereto-
fore or hereafter, by   and/or   to
the Trustees, as joint tenants or otherwise, shall be deemed trust property and Trustees agree to hold the same in trust for the purposes and on
the conditions hereinafter set forth.

2. RESERVATIONS.   and   (or
the survivor of them) reserve(s) the right to amend or revoke this trust
and Trustees agree to reassign or reconvey to them or the survivor of
them any property affected by the exercise of such right.

3. TRUSTEE. If one acting as a trustee shall become disabled as defined in the paragraph entitled "DISABILITY" in Article V, he/she shall
be deemed to have resigned.

If none of the parties is acting as a trustee, the personal representative of the last to act or, if he has none appointed within thirty (30) days
after he ceases to act, East Lansing State Bank shall become trustee by
filing with a beneficiary hereunder a written acceptance of trust.

Individual trustees shall be reimbursed for their reasonable out-of-
pocket expenses, but shall receive no additional compensation for their
services. A corporate trustee shall be entitled to reimbursement for expenses and fees in accordance with its published fee schedule in effect
at the time the services for which the fee is charged are performed, and
if there is no such fee schedule then in effect, such fees as, from time to

REVOCABLE LIVING TRUST

time, are recognized in the area as ordinary and reasonable for the services it performs.

4. DISTRIBUTION.

INCOME: While both   and   are living and not disabled, all of the net income shall be paid to them or at their direction. If both of them become disabled, Trustees shall, in their discretion, apply income for their benefit or accumulate income and thereafter treat it as corpus. After the death of   or   , Trustees shall likewise pay or apply net income to or for the benefit of the survivor of them.

CORPUS: Trustees may pay to either or   ,from the corpus of the trust from time to time, such further accounts (even to the exhaustion of the trust) as in their discretion they deem necessary or advisable to properly maintain him or her in the style to which he or she is presently accustomed, and shall do so if he or she becomes disabled; such payments may include amounts to or for the benefit of persons dependent upon them for support and premiums on life insurance on either of them or such persons whether or not such policies are payable to this trust.

ON DEATH: Upon the death of   or   , Trustees shall pay the expenses of his or her last illness and burial and all debts and taxes and other charges against him or her or arising because of his or her death which shall seem proper; upon the death of the survivor of them, Trustees shall pay such expenses, debts, taxes and charges arising because of the survivor's death and shall pay over all remaining property, both corpus and accumulated income, to the issue of   and   ,surviving such survivor, per stirpes, their children to be the stock.

Notwithstanding the foregoing, if any distributee has not attained his majority, his share shall be continued in trust, with Trustees accumulating income and distributing to him so much thereof and of corpus from time to time as they deem for his best interests and welfare and upon his reaching his majority, paying over to him property, if any remaining; and, in the event of his death, paying property on hand to his personal representative.

5. MISCELLANEOUS.

SURVIVAL DEFINED. No person shall be considered to have survived another if he or she shall die within thirty (30) days after the death of the other.

DISABILITY. If two medical doctors determine that a beneficiary or a trustee is suffering from physical or mental disability to the extent he or she is incapable of exercising judgment about or attending to financial and property transactions, such determination reduced to writing and delivered to any beneficiary or contingent beneficiary under this agreement, or to another trustee, shall be conclusive for the purposes of this agreement.

REVOCABLE LIVING TRUST

6. ADMINISTRATIVE POWERS. Trustees shall have the power to retain, sell, invest and reinvest, loan, improve, lease and borrow.

7. ACCOUNTING. So long as   lives and is not disabled, Trustees need keep no accounts because of the control which he or she has retained. However, in the event of the disability or death of Trustees shall keep an account of receipts and disbursements and of property on hand at the end of the accounting period and shall deliver copies to the beneficiaries or if one is a minor, to one with whom he or she makes his home.

8. EXCULPATORY. No purchaser from or other person dealing with Trustees shall be responsible for the application of any purchase money or other thing of value paid or delivered to them, but the receipt of Trustees shall be a full discharge; and no purchaser or other person dealing with Trustees and no issuer, or transfer agent or other agent of any issuer of any securities to which any dealing with Trustees should relate, shall be under any obligation to ascertain or inquire into the power of trustees to purchase, sell, exchange, transfer, mortgage, pledge, lease, distribute or otherwise in any manner dispose of or deal with any security or any other property held by Trustees or comprised in the trust estate.

The certificate of the Trustees that they are acting according to the terms of this instrument shall fully protect all persons dealing with Trustees.

9. CONFLICT OF LAWS. All questions concerning the validity, construction and administration of the trust shall be determined under the laws of the State of Michigan.

IN WITNESS WHEREOF, the parties have executed this instrument.

Date: _____

Witness:

_____   _____

_____   _____

STATE OF MICHIGAN } SS.
COUNTY OF

On   before me, a Notary Public, in and for said County, personally appeared   and   to me known to be the same persons described in and who executed the within instrument, who acknowledged the same to be their free act and deed.

Prepared by: _____

_____   , Notary Public

_____   County, Michigan

My Commission Expires:

DOMESTIC PARTNERSHIP AGREEMENT

This AGREEMENT is made on the date set forth below between and , hereafter referred to as the parties.

RECITALS

WHEREAS the parties live together and intend to continue living together until either decides to terminate the cohabitation;

WHEREAS, the parties intend and plan to participate in a marriage ceremony within several weeks after the date hereof and thereafter to behave towards each other in all manners as if married;

WHEREAS, each party owns substantial assets consisting of both real and/or personal property;

WHEREAS, each party desires to set forth their mutual agreement and understanding in writing, including agreements by the parties regarding property held by each, payment of expenses during cohabitation, rights to support by one of the other, possession of the cohabited premises, and certain other concerns of the parties hereto.

NOW THEREFORE, the parties hereto for good and valuable consideration, and the mutual covenants and agreements herein contained, hereby mutually agree and covenant as follows:

1. The aforesaid recitals and statements are true and correct in all material respects.

2. Each clause of this AGREEMENT is separate and divisible from the others, and, should a court refuse to enforce one or more clauses of this AGREEMENT, the others are still valid and in full force.

3. The parties live together and plan to continue to do so indefinitely.

4. The parties agree that all of each party's "Separate Property," as herein defined, whether real or personal, is the exclusive property of each party and that such property and the rents, issues and profits from it are the sole and separate property of the party who owns it, and that neither party has acquired an interest or shall acquire any right to or interest in that property or the rents, issues and profits from it by virtue of the parties' cohabitation or any other circumstance, except as provided herein.

For all purposes of this AGREEMENT, and as used herein, the term "Separate Property" shall mean, with respect to a party hereto, all of such party's right, title, and interest, legal or beneficial, in and to any and all property and interests in property, real, personal, or mixed, wherever situated, and regardless of whether now owned or hereafter acquired including, but not limited to, property inherited by a party, property gifted to a party by a third party and property which will be transferred by a third party in fulfillment of a legal obligation.

5. The earnings and income resulting from personal services after the date of execution of this AGREEMENT shall remain the separate property of the party whose services are compensated.

DOMESTIC PARTNERSHIP AGREEMENT

6. All property received by either party by gift, descent or devise shall remain the sole and separate property of the party receiving it, and the other party shall have no right to or claim in said property by virtue of the parties' cohabitation or any other circumstance.

7. The parties shall be jointly responsible for basic living expenses. Such expenses include, and are limited to: rent or mortgage, if any, utilities (including electricity, gas, water), telephone (excluding long distance charges which shall be allocable to the party who made or received the calls), real property tax, home owner's insurance, food and beverages. It is expressly agreed that basic living expenses for which the parties agree to be jointly responsible do not include the costs of medical care, income tax liability, or the cost of room and board of a dwelling other than the one jointly occupied by the parties.

8. In the event the parties jointly acquire any real or personal property, they shall list a full description of such property on a separate schedule which shall be maintained with records pertaining to this AGREEMENT and their cohabitation. Ownership by the parties in jointly acquired property shall be in a fifty/fifty ratio, unless otherwise noted in a writing signed by both parties.

9. The parties currently cohabit the real property located at   is the legal owner of a fifty percent tenancy in common interest in said property. It is understood and agreed that   has an equitable interest in said property.   and   are both entitled to possession of the entire property on an equal basis during the duration of their cohabitation. In the event of a separation, as defined herein, it is agreed that   will vacate the subject real property. It is further agreed that   will execute a deed and any other documents necessary to transfer his/her ownership interest in the subject property to such third party as   shall designate at the time of separation, and   shall make no claim that he/she is entitled to any interest in said property.

10. The parties agree that neither has obtained by this AGREEMENT or by the fact of cohabitation or by any other means, the right to succeed to or inherit property from the estate of the other except by valid will, or the acquisition of property in joint tenancy with right of survivorship, after the date of this AGREEMENT. The parties understand that neither is obligated to give property to the other by will or otherwise.

11. The parties agree that "separation" for purposes of this AGREEMENT shall exist when one of the parties a) delivers to the other a notice of intention to separate; and b) either vacates the cohabited premises or requests that the other party vacate the premises.

12. In the event of a separation, the parties shall equally divide all jointly held and jointly acquired property. The parties shall attempt to distribute the property to be divided in kind where feasible; property to be divided which cannot be distributed in kind shall be sold and the proceeds divided. Distribution of property, or proceeds from the sale of

DOMESTIC PARTNERSHIP AGREEMENT

property, shall be in accordance with ownership as provided in paragraphs 5., 6., 8. and 9. above.

13. It is further agreed that if during the period of cohabitation, made any payments toward repairs, renovations-or capital improvements of the real property, upon separation he/she shall be entitled to receive full reimbursement of all such payments from . The parties shall keep a written record of all such repair and/or improvement payments made by shall also be entitled to receive interest on all such payments. The interest shall be calculated based upon the cost of living in accordance with the U.S. Government COLA index, during the intervening years between the date of the repair/improvement payment and the date of separation.

14. In the event that the parties are unable to agree to a division of their jointly owned property, they shall select a panel of three arbitrators, in accordance with the procedures contained in paragraph 19 below. The arbitrators shall a) appraise the jointly owned property at fair market value and b) divide the jointly owned property as nearly equally between the two parties as possible. In the event an equal in kind division of the property is not possible, the parties agree to sell such items of their jointly owned property as the arbitrator shall select. In the event that an equal division of the property is not possible, and the parties and arbitrators agree that sale of any item of jointly owned property would be impossible or wasteful, then the arbitrator may award more than a one-half share of the property to one party in exchange for cash or a promissory note to the other party, upon reasonable terms and interest. In making such an award, the arbitrator shall take into consideration the parties' relative financial conditions.

15. In the event of a separation, the parties agree that shall pay to for a period of three months following the date vacates the shared real property, any and all rental income received from the rear cottage located at the above property. With the exception of this payment of rental income, it is agreed that neither party has any right to support or other compensation from the other party in consequence of cohabitation or this AGREEMENT.

16. In the event of a separation, the parties agree that they shall each return to the other any and all letters written by the other.

17. In the event of a separation, it is agreed that shall not write or publish any articles, stories or other writing about or about his/her relationship with

18. In the event of a separation, agrees that he/she is not entitled to receive any motor vehicles acquired during the relationship, unless he/she is the registered owner of the vehicle.

DOMESTIC PARTNERSHIP AGREEMENT

19. Each party covenants and agrees that any dispute pertaining to this AGREEMENT which arises between them shall be submitted to binding arbitration according to the following procedures:

a. The request for arbitration may be made by either party and shall be in writing and delivered to the other party;

b. Pending the outcome of arbitration, there shall be no change made in the language of the AGREEMENT;

c. The arbitration panel that will resolve any disputes regarding the AGREEMENT shall consist of three persons: one person chosen by   , one person chosen by   , and one person chosen by the other panel members so selected.

d. Within fourteen days following the breakdown of mediation, the arbitrators shall be chosen;

e. Within fourteen days following the selection of all members of the arbitration panel, the panel will hear the dispute between the parties;

f. Within seven days subsequent to the hearing, the arbitration panel will make a decision and communicate it in writing to each party.

20. If a party institutes legal action to enforce his/her rights under this AGREEMENT, or to have a court determine the meaning of a dispute term, the prevailing party shall be entitled to reasonable attorneys' fees as fixed by the court. Notwithstanding the above, no party who fails or refuses to submit a dispute for resolution pursuant to the provisions of paragraph 19. above, shall be entitled to attorneys' fees in any legal action in which such dispute is all or part of the cause of action being sued upon.

21. Each party agrees that all questions with respect to the interpretation and enforcement of this AGREEMENT shall be resolved pursuant to the laws of the State of California.

22. Each party acknowledges and agrees that he/she signed this AGREEMENT voluntarily and freely, of his/her own choice, without any duress of any kind whatsoever.

23. This AGREEMENT contains the entire understanding of the parties. There are no promises, understandings, agreements or representations between the parties other than those expressly stated in this AGREEMENT.

24. This AGREEMENT may be altered or amended only by written agreement signed by both parties.

DOMESTIC PARTNERSHIP AGREEMENT

25. Each party further acknowledges that this AGREEMENT was drafted by _____, Attorney At Law, at the request of both parties; that they were advised that they might be waiving valuable rights by signing this AGREEMENT; that each party has been advised to seek the advice of separate counsel of his/her own choosing; and that each party understands the meaning and significance of each provision of this AGREEMENT, the force and effect of each such provision having been explained prior to execution of this AGREEMENT.

IN WITNESS WHEREOF, the parties hereunto have executed this AGREEMENT, in the City and County of San Francisco, California, on the date set forth below.

_____

Date: _____   _____

On _____ before me, a Notary Public in and for said State, personally appeared   and _____ known to me to be the persons whose names are subscribed to the within AGREEMENT, and acknowledged that they executed the same to be their free act and deed.

_____
, Notary Public
San Francisco County, California
My Commission Expires: _____

Prepared by:

_____

_____

FINANCIAL POWER OF ATTORNEY
(Effective Immediately)

I,_____ , the principal, of
_____ make this power of attorney according to sec. 495 of the Revised Probate Code of Michigan. I also revoke any prior power of attorney I may have made dealing with my financial affairs as described below.

1. APPOINTMENT OF AGENT.

I appoint_____ of
_____ as my agent.

If that person fails, for any reason, to serve as my agent, I appoint as successor agent _____ of
_____ .

2. DURATION. This power of attorney shall take effect when I sign it. This power of attorney shall not be affected by my disability.

3. POWERS OF AGENT. Except as stated in paragraph 4, the agent can do anything with regard to my financial affairs that I could do, including powers to:

(a)*Property management.* Buy, sell, give (outright or in trust), hold, convey, exchange, lease, partition, improve, mortgage, option, insure, invest or otherwise deal with my real or personal property (my real property may be described in an attachment to this form, which may be revised from time to time). Make deeds, bills of sale, purchase agreements, land contracts, sales contracts, listing agreements, easements, mortgages, leases, options, security agreements or other documents with regard to my real or personal property.

(b) *Investment.* Invest or reinvest in stocks, bonds, loans, U.S. government obligations (including savings bonds and treasury bills) and other securities; receive dividends or interest from the securities; vote stock in person or by proxy; deal with the securities directly or through a brokerage firm; make any documents with regard to the securities.

(c)*Business manage.* Operate, participate in, reorganize, recapitalize, incorporate, sell, consolidate, merge, close, liquidate or dissolve a business that I might be engaged in; employ agents, officers or directors for the business; make contracts with regard to the business, including buy-sell or partnership agreements.

(d) *Borrowing.* Borrow money, unsecured or secured by my property; make promissory notes, mortgages, security agreements, guaranties or similar documents in connection with any borrowing.

(e)*Debts and expenses.* Pay bills, loans, notes or other debts owed by me or incurred by the agent on my behalf; pay all expenses for the support and maintenance of me or my dependents; pay all expenses for the management of my property.

FINANCIAL POWER OF ATTORNEY

(f) *Financial institutions.* Open or close an account at a bank, savings and loan association, credit union or other financial institution; make deposits or withdrawals from the account, and make drafts, checks, receipts, notes or other instruments for that purpose; lease, discontinue, enter or withdraw contents from a safe deposit box at a financial institution; carry on any other transactions at financial institutions.

(g) *Taxes.* Pay federal, state or local taxes I owe, or any interest or penalty on them; make and file tax returns, reports, forms, declarations or other documents for these taxes; claim and cash any tax refund; handle any and all federal, state and local tax matters.

(h) *Employee benefits.* Exercise all rights, options, powers or privileges for any pension, thrift, stock option or ownership, profit-sharing or other employee benefit plan I am eligible for.

(i) *Government benefits.* Apply for and receive any government benefits, including social security, that I am eligible for; receive and cash or deposit any benefit check or draft.

(j) *Legal and administrative proceedings.* Begin, continue, defend, appeal, settle or compromise any legal or administrative proceedings involving me or my property.

(k) *Insurance.* Obtain, redeem, borrow against, amend, cancel, convert, pledge, surrender or change any insurance I have; make any documents, forms or affidavits in connection with any insurance.

(l) M*otor vehicles.* Apply for or transfer the certificates of title to automobiles or other motor vehicles.

(m) *Agents and employees.* Employ and compensate real estate brokers, stockbrokers, investment advisers, accountants, lawyers, or other agents and employees.

(n) *Other powers.* I also give the agent powers to:

4. RESTRICTIONS ON POWERS OF AGENT. The agent shall not have the power to do any of the following things: a) make a will or codicil for me, b) change the beneficiary of any life insurance, c) have any power or incidents of ownership over life insurance I own on the agent's life, d) exercise any powers that would make my property taxable to the agent for income, gift, estate or inheritance tax purposes, e) other:

_____

_____

5. COMPENSATION OF AGENT. The agent may receive reimbursement for actual and necessary expenses incurred in carrying out the above powers. Otherwise, the agent shall not receive any compensation.

FINANCIAL POWER OF ATTORNEY

6. RELIANCE BY THIRD PARTIES. Third parties can rely on this power of attorney or the agent's representations about it. Anyone who does shall not be liable to me for permitting the agent to exercise powers under the power of attorney, unless they have actual knowledge that the power of attorney has terminated.

7. MISCELLANEOUS. This power of attorney shall be governed by Michigan law, although it may be used out of state. Photocopies of this document shall have the same legal authority as the original.

I sign my name to this power of attorney on _____
19_____

_____
Principal

Witnesses:

_____

_____

STATE OF MICHIGAN
COUNTY OF _____ } SS.

This instrument was acknowledged before me on _____ 19____ by _____

_____
Notary Public
_____County, Michigan
My commission expires _____

Prepared by:

_____

_____

FINANCIAL POWER OF ATTORNEY
(Effective on Disability)

I,_____ , the principal, of
_____ make this power of attorney
according to sec. 495 of the Revised Probate Code of Michigan. I also
revoke any prior power of attorney I may have made dealing with my
financial affairs as described below.

1. APPOINTMENT OF AGENT.

I appoint_____ of
_____ as my agent.

If that person fails, for any reason, to serve as my agent, I appoint as
successor agent _____ of
_____ .

2. DURATION. This power of attorney shall take effect upon my disability. For the purpose of this power of attorney, I shall be disabled
when I am unable to manage my personal and financial affairs. That
determination shall be made, in writing, by a physician. Recovery from
disability shall be determined in the same manner.

If possible, the physician determining my disability or recovery from
a disability shall be _____ of
_____ .

3. POWERS OF AGENT. Except as stated in paragraph 4, the agent
can do anything with regard to my financial affairs that I could do, including powers to:

(a)*Property management.* Buy, sell, give (outright or in trust),
hold, convey, exchange, lease, partition, improve, mortgage, option, insure, invest or otherwise deal with my real or personal
property (my real property may be described in an attachment
to this form, which may be revised from time to time). Make
deeds, bills of sale, purchase agreements, land contracts, sales
contracts, listing agreements, easements, mortgages, leases, options, security agreements or other documents with regard to my
real or personal property.

(b) *Investment.* Invest or reinvest in stocks, bonds, loans, U.S.
government obligations (including savings bonds and treasury
bills) and other securities; receive dividends or interest from the
securities; vote stock in person or by proxy; deal with the securities directly or through a brokerage firm; make any documents
with regard to the securities.

(c)*Business manage.* Operate, participate in, reorganize, recapitalize, incorporate, sell, consolidate, merge, close, liquidate or
dissolve a business that I might be engaged in; employ agents,
officers or directors for the business; make contracts with regard
to the business, including buy-sell or partnership agreements.

(d) *Borrowing.* Borrow money, unsecured or secured by my
property; make promissory notes, mortgages, security agreements, guaranties or similar documents in connection with any
borrowing.

FINANCIAL POWER OF ATTORNEY

(e)*Debts and expenses*. Pay bills, loans, notes or other debts owed by me or incurred by the agent on my behalf; pay all expenses for the support and maintenance of me or my dependents; pay all expenses for the management of my property.

(f) *Financial institutions*. Open or close an account at a bank, savings and loan association, credit union or other financial institution; make deposits or withdrawals from the account, and make drafts, checks, receipts, notes or other instruments for that purpose; lease, discontinue, enter or withdraw contents from a safe deposit box at a financial institution; carry on any other transactions at financial institutions.

(g) *Taxes*. Pay federal, state or local taxes I owe, or any interest or penalty on them; make and file tax returns, reports, forms, declarations or other documents for these taxes; claim and cash any tax refund; handle any and all federal, state and local tax matters.

(h) *Employee benefits*. Exercise all rights, options, powers or privileges for any pension, thrift, stock option or ownership, profit-sharing or other employee benefit plan I am eligible for.

(i) *Government benefits*. Apply for and receive any government benefits, including social security, that I am eligible for; receive and cash or deposit any benefit check or draft.

(j) *Legal and administrative proceedings*. Begin, continue, defend, appeal, settle or compromise any legal or administrative proceedings involving me or my property.

(k) *Insurance*. Obtain, redeem, borrow against, amend, cancel, convert, pledge, surrender or change any insurance I have; make any documents, forms or affidavits in connection with any insurance.

(l) *Motor vehicles*. Apply for or transfer the certificates of title to automobiles or other motor vehicles.

(m) *Agents and employees*. Employ and compensate real estate brokers, stockbrokers, investment advisers, accountants, lawyers, or other agents and employees.

(n) *Other powers*. I also give the agent powers to:

_____

_____

4. RESTRICTIONS ON POWERS OF AGENT. The agent shall not have the power to do any of the following things: a) make a will or codicil for me, b) change the beneficiary of any life insurance, c) have any power or incidents of ownership over life insurance I own on the agent's life, d) exercise any powers that would make my property taxable to the agent for income, gift, estate or inheritance tax purposes, e) other:

_____

_____

FINANCIAL POWER OF ATTORNEY

5. COMPENSATION OF AGENT. The agent may receive reimbursement for actual and necessary expenses incurred in carrying out the above powers. Otherwise, the agent shall not receive any compensation.

6. RELIANCE BY THIRD PARTIES. Third parties can rely on this power of attorney or the agent's representations about it. Anyone who does shall not be liable to me for permitting the agent to exercise powers under the power of attorney, unless they have actual knowledge that the power of attorney has terminated.

7. MISCELLANEOUS. This power of attorney shall be governed by Michigan law, although it may be used out of state. Photocopies of this document shall have the same legal authority as the original.

I sign my name to this power of attorney on _____
19_____

_____
Principal

Witnesses:

_____

_____

STATE OF MICHIGAN
COUNTY OF _____ } SS.

This instrument was acknowledged before me on _____ 19____ by _____

_____
Notary Public

_____County, Michigan

My commission expires _____

Prepared by:

_____

_____

PHYSICIAN'S STATEMENT

I, _____ of
_____ am a physician.

I have examined the principal and it is my opinion that he/she is unable to manage his/her personal and financial affairs.

_____   _____
Date   Physician

LIMITED FINANCIAL POWER OF ATTORNEY

I, _____ , the principal, of
_____ make this power of attorney
according to sec. 495 of the Revised Probate Code of Michigan. I also
revoke any prior power of attorney I may have made dealing with my
financial affairs as described below.

1. APPOINTMENT OF AGENT.

I appoint _____ of
_____ as my agent.

If that person fails, for any reason, to serve as my agent, I appoint as
successor agent _____ of
_____ .

2. DURATION. This power of attorney shall take effect when I sign
it. The power of attorney shall not be affected by my disability.

3. POWERS OF AGENT. The agent can do the following thing(s) for
me:

_____

_____

If I have given the agent the power to transfer real property, the property may be described in an attachment to this form, which may be revised from time to time.

5. COMPENSATION OF AGENT. The agent may receive reimbursement for actual and necessary expenses incurred in carrying out the above
powers. Otherwise, the agent shall not receive any compensation.

6. RELIANCE BY THIRD PARTIES. Third parties can rely on this
power of attorney or the agent's representations about it. Anyone who
does shall not be liable to me for permitting the agent to exercise powers
under the power of attorney, unless they have actual knowledge that the
power of attorney has terminated.

7. MISCELLANEOUS. This power of attorney shall be governed by
Michigan law, although it may be used out of state. Photocopies of this
document shall have the same legal authority as the original.

I sign my name to this power of attorney on _____
19_____ .

_____
Principal

Witnesses:

_____

_____

LIMITED FINANCIAL POWER OF ATTORNEY

STATE OF MICHIGAN
COUNTY OF _____ } SS.

This instrument was acknowledged before me on
_____ 19 _____ by _____ .

_____
Notary Public
_____ County, Michigan
My commission expires _____

Prepared by:

_____

_____

REVOCATION OF POWER OF ATTORNEY

I,_____, the principal, of
_____ revoke my power of attorney
dated _____ [and recorded on _____ , at Liber
_____, Page _____ , in the office of the Register of Deeds,
_____ County, Michigan], and all the powers given
to my agent _____ in such power of attorney.

_____   _____
Date   Principal

Witnesses:

_____

_____

STATE OF MICHIGAN   } SS.
COUNTY OF _____

This instrument was acknowledged before me on
_____ 19 _____ by _____ .

_____
Notary Public
_____ County, Michigan
My commission expires _____

Prepared by:

_____

_____

LIVING WILL

Being of sound mind, I willfully and voluntarily hereby make known my desire that my dying shall not be artificially prolonged under the circumstances set forth below.

If at any time I should have an incurable injury, disease, or illness, regarded as a terminal condition by my physician, and if my physician has determined that the application of life-sustaining procedures would serve only to artificially prolong the dying process and that my death will occur whether or not life-sustaining procedures are utilized, I direct that such procedures be withheld or withdrawn and that I be permitted to die with only the administration of medication or the performance of any medical procedure deemed necessary to provide me with comfort care.

In the absence of my ability to give directions regarding the use of such life-sustaining procedures, it is my intention that this declaration should be honored by my family and physician as the final expression of my legal right to refuse medical or surgical treatment and to accept the consequences of such refusal.

I understand the full import of this declaration, and I am emotionally and mentally competent to make this declaration.

_____   _____
Date   (Declarant)

The declarant has been personally known to me, and I believe him or her to be of sound mind.

Witness:_____ Witness: _____

Subscribed and sworn to before me on the _____ day of _____, 19____

_____

Notary Public, State of _____

My commission expires _____

MEDICAL POWER OF ATTORNEY

I,_____ , the patient, of
_____ make this power of attorney
according to secs. 495 and 496 of the Revised Probate Code of Michigan.
I also revoke any prior power of attorney I may have made dealing with
my health care as described below.

1. DESIGNATION OF PATIENT ADVOCATE.

I designate _____ of
_____ as my patient advocate.

If that person fails, for any reason, to serve as my agent, I designate
as successor patient advocate _____ of
_____.

2. DURATION. This power of attorney shall take effect only when I
am unable to participate in medical treatment decisions. That determination shall be made, in writing, by my attending physician and another
physician or licensed psychologist. This power of attorney shall not be
affected by my disability.

3. POWERS OF PATIENT ADVOCATE. Except as prohibited by law
or as restricted in paragraph 5, the patient advocate shall make all decisions about my care, custody and medical treatment, including powers
to:

(a) have access to medical records and information; give medical waivers and authorizations.

(b) authorize admission to or discharge from health care fa-
cilities, including hospitals, hospices and nursing homes

(c) employ or discharge medical caregivers, including physicians, nurses and therapists, and pay them reasonable compensation from my funds

(d) consent to or refuse any medical treatment, including di-
agnostic, surgical and therapeutic procedures

4. FOREGOING LIFE-SUSTAINING TREATMENT (OPTIONAL). By
signing below this paragraph, I give the patient advocate the power to
decide to withhold or withdraw treatment that would allow me to die. I
acknowledge that such a decision could or would allow my death.

_____
Patient

5. Exercise of Powers. In exercising the above powers, the patient
advocate shall make decisions according to my best interests, or as in-
structed by me orally or in writing below:

_____

_____

6. RELIANCE BY THIRD PARTIES. Third parties can rely on this
power of attorney, the doctors' statement or the patient advocate's rep-

MEDICAL POWER OF ATTORNEY

resentations about them. Anyone who does shall not be liable to me for permitting the patient advocate to exercise powers under the power of attorney, unless they have actual knowledge that the power of attorney has been revoked.

7. MISCELLANEOUS. This power of attorney shall be governed by Michigan law, although it may be used out of state. Photocopies of this document shall have the same legal authority as the original.

I am 18 years of age or older and of sound mind. I am signing this power of attorney voluntarily and without undue influence, duress or fraud.

I sign my name to this power of attorney on _____
19_____

_____
Patient

STATEMENT OF WITNESSES

We are eligible to serve as witnesses. We have witnessed the patient's signature, and state that the patient appears to be of sound mind and under no undue influence, duress or fraud.

_____
Signature of Witness

_____
Name of Witness

_____
City   State   Zip

_____
Signature of Witness

_____
Name of Witness

_____
City   State   Zip

_____
Signature of Witness

_____
Name of Witness

_____
City   State   Zip

MEDICAL POWER OF ATTORNEY

DOCTORS' STATEMENT

I,_____ of
_____ am the patient's attending
physician.

I,_____ of
_____ am either a physician or a
licensed psychologist.

We have examined the patient and it is our opinion that he/she is
unable to participate in medical treatment decisions.

_____   _____

Date   Physician

_____   _____

Date   Physician

ACCEPTANCE OF DESIGNATION

I have been designated as the patient advocate of the patient making
this power of attorney. I accept that designation and agree to act as required by law and as stated below:

(a) This designation shall not become effective unless the patient is unable to participate in medical treatment decisions.

(b) A patient advocate shall not exercise powers concerning
the patient's care, custody, and medical treatment that the patient, if the patient were able participate in the decision, could
not have exercised on his or her own behalf.

(c) This designation cannot be used to make a medical treatment decision to withhold or withdraw treatment from a patient
who is pregnant that would result in the pregnant patient's death.

(d) A patient advocate may make a decision to withhold or
withdraw treatment which would allow a patient to die only if
the patient has expressed in a clear and convincing manner that
the patient advocate is authorized to make such a decision, and
that the patient acknowledges that such a decision could or would
allow the patient's death.

(e) A patient advocate shall not receive compensation for the
performance of his or her authority, rights, and responsibilities,
but a patient advocate may be reimbursed for actual and necessary expenses incurred in the performance of his or her authority, rights, and responsibilities.

MEDICAL POWER OF ATTORNEY

(f) A patient advocate shall act in accordance with the standards of care applicable to fiduciaries when acting for the patient and shall act consistent with the patient's best interests. The known desires of the patient expressed or evidenced while the patient is able to participate in medical treatment decisions are presumed to be in the patient's best interests.

(g) A patient may revoke his or her designation at any time and in any manner sufficient to communicate an intent to revoke.

(h) A patient advocate may revoke his or her acceptance to the designation at any time and in any manner sufficient to communicate an intent to revoke.

(i) A patient admitted to a health facility or agency has the rights enumerated in section 20201 of the public health code, Act. No. 368 of the Public Acts of 1978, being section 333.20201 of the Michigan Compiled Laws.

_____   _____
Date   Patient Advocate

LETTER OF INSTRUCTION

This version of a letter of instruction, adapted from a form provided by Citibank, suggests the various items and the level of detail that should be specified, but you should feel free to adapt it to your own situation and the nature of your assets. People who make frequent changes in their securities or their insurance policies may find that a loose-leaf binder or a box of index cards is more convenient and more flexible.

Name: _____

YOU CAN EXPECT

From my employer: _____
(Person to contact, dept., phone)

_____
(life insurance)   (profit sharing)

_____
(accident insurance)   (pension plan)

_____
(other benefits)

From insurance companies: _____
(total amount)

From Social Security: _____
(lump sum plus monthly benefits)

From the Veterans Administration: _____
(you must inform VA)

From other sources:_____

UPDATED_____
(date)

FIRST THINGS TO DO

1. Call _____ to help.
(relative or friend)

2. Notify my employer: _____
(phone)

3. Make arrangements with funeral home. See page _____

4. Request at least 5 copies of the death certificate. (Usually, the funeral director will get them).

5. Call our lawyer: _____
(name, phone)

LETTER OF INSTRUCTION

6. Contact local Social Security office.
7. Get and process my insurance policies.
8. Notify bank that holds our home mortgage.

SOCIAL SECURITY

Name: _____ Soc. Sec. number:_____

Location of card: _____

File a claim immediately to avoid possibility of losing any benefit checks.

Call local Social Security office for appointment. They tell you what to bring. _____

(phone)

Expect a lump sum of about $_____, plus continuing benefits for children under 18, or until 22 for full-time students.

A spouse may receive benefits until children reach 18, between ages 50-60 if disabled, or if over 60.

SAFE DEPOSIT BOX*

Bank: _____

Address: _____

In whose name: _____ Number:_____

Location of key: _____

List of contents: _____

POST OFFICE BOX

Address:_____

Owners:_____

Number:_____

Location of key/combin. _____

*In the event of death, the bank may be required by state law to seal the lessee's box as soon as notified, even if jointly leased.

LOCATION OF PERSONAL PAPERS

Last will and testament: _____

Birth and baptismal certificates: _____

Communion and confirmation certificates: _____

School diplomas: _____

Marriage certificate: _____

Military records: _____

LETTER OF INSTRUCTION

Naturalization Papers:_____

Other (adoption, etc.): _____

CHECKING ACCOUNTS

Bank: _____

Address:_____

Name(s) on account: _____

Account number: _____

Kind of account: _____

Repeat to cover all accounts of husband and wife.

Canceled checks and statements are in: _____
(location)

SAVINGS ACCOUNTS AND CERTIFICATES

Bank: _____

Address:_____

Name(s) on account: _____

Account number: _____

Kind of account: _____ Type: _____

Location of passbook (or certificate receipt): _____

Any special instructions: _____

Repeat for each account.

DOCTORS' NAMES/ADDRESSES

Doctor(s): _____
(name, address, phone, whose doctor)

Dentist(s): _____

Pediatrician:_____

Children's dentist: _____

CREDIT CARDS

All credit cards in my name should be canceled or converted to your name.

Company: _____ Phone:_____

Address_____

Name on card:_____ Number: _____

Location of card: _____

Repeat for each card.

LETTER OF INSTRUCTION

LOANS OUTSTANDING
(OTHER THAN MORTGAGES)

Bank:_____

Address:_____

Name on loan:_____

Account number:_____

Monthly payment: _____

Location of papers:_____

(and payment book, if any)

Collateral, if any: _____

Life insurance on loan? ☐ (yes) ☐ (no)

Repeat for all loans

DEBTS OWED TO ME

Debtor: _____

Description: _____

Terms: _____

Balance: _____

Location of documents _____

CAR

Year, make, and model: _____

Identification number: _____

Location of papers: _____

(title, registration)

Repeat for each car.

INCOME TAX RETURNS

Location of all previous returns—federal, state, local:

_____

Our tax preparer: _____

(name, address, phone)

Check: Are estimated quarterly taxes due?

LETTER OF INSTRUCTION

SPECIAL WISHES

1. _____

2. _____

PERSONAL EFFECTS

I would like certain people to be given these personal effects

Person

My white jade pendant _____

My camera _____

My photography books _____

All my other books _____

Other items _____

INVESTMENTS

Stocks

Company: _____

Name on certificate(s): _____

Number of shares: _____

Purchase price and date: _____

Location of certificate(s): _____

Repeat for each investment

Bonds/Notes/Bills

Issuer: _____

Issued to: _____

(owner)

Face amount:_____ Bond number: _____

Purchase price and date: _____

Maturity date: _____

Location of certificate(s): _____

Mutual Funds

Company:_____

Name on account: _____

No. of shares or units: _____

Location of statement(s), certificate(s): _____

Other Investments (U.S. savings bonds, etc.)

For each, list amount invested; to whom issued; issuer; maturity date and other applicable date; location of certificates and other vital papers.

LETTER OF INSTRUCTION

CEMETERY AND FUNERAL

Cemetery Plot

Location: _____

When purchased: _____

Deed number: _____

Location of deed: _____

Other information: _____

(perpetual care, etc.)

Facts for Funeral Director (Bring this with you, and bring cemetery deed, if possible)

My Full Name: _____

Residence: _____ Phone: _____

Marital status: _____ Spouse: _____

Date of Birth: _____ Birthplace: _____

Father's name and birthplace: _____

Mother's maiden name: _____

Length of residence in state: _____ In U.S.: _____

Military service: ☐ (yes) ☐ (no) When: _____

(Bring veterans' discharge papers if possible.)

Social Security number: _____ Occupation: _____

Life insurance (bring policy if proceeds will be used for funeral expenses):

_____

(company names and policy numbers)

LIFE INSURANCE

Location of all policies: _____

To collect benefits, a copy of the death certificate must be sent to each company.

Policy: _____

(amount)

Whose life is insured: _____

Insurance company: _____

Company address: _____

Kind of policy: _____ Policy number: _____

Beneficiaries: _____

Issue date: _____ Maturity date: _____

How paid out: _____

LETTER OF INSTRUCTION

Your other options on payout: _____
Other special facts: _____
Repeat information above for each policy.
For _____ in veterans' insurance call
    (amount)
local Veterans Administration office: _____
                                    (phone)

OTHER INSURANCE

Accident
Company: _____
Address: _____
Policy number: _____
Beneficiaries: _____
Coverage: _____
Location of Policy: _____
Agent, if any: _____
Car, Home and Household
Give information below for each policy.
Coverage: _____
Company: _____
Address: _____
Policy number: _____
Location of policy: _____
Term (when to renew): _____
Agent, if any: _____
Medical
Coverage: _____
Company: _____
Address: _____
Policy number: _____
Location of policy: _____
Through employer or other group: _____
Agent, if any: _____
Repeat for all medical insurance policies.
Mortgage Insurance: See page _____.

LETTER OF INSTRUCTION

HOUSE, CONDO, OR CO-OP

In whose name: _____

Address: _____

Lot: _____ Block: _____ On map called; _____

Other descriptions needed: _____

Our lawyer at closing: _____

(name)   (address)

Location of statement of closing, policy of title insurance, deed, land survey, etc.: _____

Mortgage

Held by: _____

(bank)

Amount of original mortgage: _____

Date taken out: _____

Amount owed now: _____

Method of payment: _____

Location of payment book, if any (or payment statements):

_____

Life insurance on mortgage ☐ (yes) ☐ (no)

If yes, policy number: _____

Location of policy: _____

Notify bank of my death; the unpaid amount will be paid automatically by the insurance, and the house is owned free and clear.

Veterans' exemption claim, if any: _____

Location of documentation papers: _____

Annual amount; _____

Contact local tax assessor for documentation needed or more information.

House Taxes

Amount: _____

Location of receipts: _____

Cost of House

Initial buying price: _____

Purchase closing fee: _____

Other costs to buy (real estate agent, legal, taxes, etc.):

_____

Improvements as of _____ come to _____

(date)   (total so far)

LETTER OF INSTRUCTION

Itemized House Improvements

Improvement: _____ Cost: _____ Date: _____

Location of bills: _____

If Renting: ☐ (yes) ☐ (no)

Lease location: _____ Expires: _____

(date)

HOUSEHOLD CONTENTS

Names of owners: _____

Form of ownership: _____

Location of documents: _____

Location of inventory: _____

IMPORTANT WARRANTIES, RECEIPTS

Item: _____

_____

(warranty location)   (receipt location)

By completing the donor card in the presence of your family and having them sign as witnesses, you'll know they pledge their support to see that your wishes are carried out. The donor card is your commitment to share life will serve as a reminder to your family and medical staff. Remember to carry it in your wallet or purse at all times.

MY COMMITMENT TO SHARE LIFE
PRINT & SIGN THIS UNIFORM DONOR CARD

I, _____, have spoken to my family about organ and tissue donation. The following people have witnessed my commitment to be a donor. I wish to donate the following:

[ ] any needed organs and tissue.
[ ] only the following organs and tissue: _____

Donor Signature _____ Date ____ / ____ / ____

Witness _____

Witness _____